AMERICA

STUDY GUIDE

TINDALL'S

AMERICA

A NARRATIVE HISTORY

STUDY GUIDE

VOLUME II

THOMAS S. MORGAN
WINTHROP COLLEGE

W · W · NORTON & COMPANY · NEW YORK · LONDON

FIRST EDITION

ISBN 0-393-95439-0

Cover Illustration:
Edward Hopper. *Queensborough Bridge*. 1913. Oil on canvas. 25½ x 37½ inches. Collection of Whitney Museum of American Art. Bequest of Josephine N. Hopper. Acq#70.1184

W. W. Norton & Company, Inc.,
500 Fifth Avenue, New York, N.Y. 10110

W. W. Norton & Company Ltd.,
37 Great Russell Street, London WC1B 3NU

2 3 4 5 6 7 8 9 0

CONTENTS

INTRODUCTION

This *Study Guide* is designed to help you learn the important concepts in *America: A Narrative History*, by George B. Tindall. It is not intended as a replacement for the textbook, but as an aid to be used along with the text. When used conscientiously, this *Study Guide* will help you to understand the major themes in American history and to do well on quizzes based on your reading.

STRUCTURE OF THIS STUDY GUIDE

Each chapter of the *Study Guide* contains the following sections:

Chapter Objectives
Chapter Outline
Key Items of Chronology
Terms to Master
Vocabulary Building
Exercises for Understanding:
    Multiple-Choice Questions
    True-False Questions
    Essay Questions
Document(s) or Reading(s)

The purpose of each of the sections, along with instructions for its use, is explained below.

Chapter Objectives

For each chapter you will find about five objectives, or key concepts, on which you should focus your attention as you read. You should read the whole of each chapter, taking in details as well as major themes, but by keeping the chapter objectives in mind you will avoid getting bogged down and missing the key ideas.

Chapter Outline

Skim this outline carefully before you begin reading a chapter. The outline provides a more detailed overview than do the objectives. Often headings in the outline are worded to suggest questions about the material. For example, "Duties of the King" and "Patterns of Colonization" raise the questions "What were the duties of the king?" and "What were the patterns of colonization?" Look for the answers to such questions as you read the text. This approach will help those of you who are new to reading history.

Key Items of Chronology

Each chapter of this *Study Guide* will include a list of dates. You need not learn every date you encounter in the chapter, but if you learn the key ones listed here and any other dates emphasized by your instructor, you will have the sound chronological framework so important for understanding historical events.

Keep in mind that dates, while important, are not the sole subject matter of history. Seldom will any of the quizzes in this *Study Guide* ask for recall of dates. On the other hand, answers to essay questions, and term papers, should include important dates and show that you are familiar with the chronology of your subject.

Terms to Master

This section of the *Study Guide* gives you a list of important terms to study. (Remember, of course, that your instructor may emphasize additional terms which you should learn.) After reading each chapter, return to the list of terms and write a brief definition of each. If you cannot recall the term readily, turn to the relevant pages in the textbook and re-read the discussion of the term. If you need or want to consult another source, go to the annotated bibliography at the end of the relevant chapter, or ask your instructor for suggestions.

Vocabulary Building

This is a section of the *Study Guide* that you may or may not need. If you do not know the meaning of the words or terms listed in Vocabulary Building, look them up in a dictionary before you begin reading a chapter. By looking up such words and then using them yourself, you will increase your vocabulary.

When the terms in Vocabulary Building are not readily found in the standard dictionary or when their use in the Tindall text lends them a special meaning, I have defined them for you. I've used the *American Heritage Dictionary*, Second College Edition, as a guide to determine which terms should be defined here for you.

Exercises for Understanding

You should reserve these exercises to use as a check on your reading after you study the chapter. The multiple-choice and true-false questions included here will test your recall and understanding of the facts in the chapter. The answers to these questions are found at the end of each *Study Guide* chapter.

Essay Questions

The essay questions which come next may be used in several ways. If you are using this *Study Guide* entirely on your own, you should try to outline answers to these questions based on your reading of the chapter. In the early stages of the course you may want to consider writing formal answers to these essay questions just as you would if you encountered them on an exam. The questions will often be quite broad and will lead you to think about material in the chapter in different ways. By reviewing the essay questions in this *Study Guide* before attending class, you will better understand the class lecture or discussion.

Documents and Readings

All the chapters in this *Study Guide* contain a section of documents or readings. The documents are sources from the time period of the chapter (primary sources), chosen to illumine some aspect of the period covered in the text. The readings are excerpts from works of historians (secondary sources), chosen either to illustrate the approach of a master historian or to offer varying interpretations of an event. Study the document or reading after you have completed the chapter, and consult the headnotes given in this *Study Guide* before each document. Then attempt to answer the questions which follow the document.

STUDYING HISTORY

The term "history" has been defined in many ways. One way to define it is "everything that has happened in the past." But there are serious problems with this definition. First, it is simply impossible to recount *everything* that has happened in the past. Any single event, such as your eating dinner, is a combination of an infinite number of subevents, ranging from the cultivation of vegetables to the mechanisms involved in digestion. Each of these is itself composed of an unlimited number of subevents. The past, which includes everything that has happened, is shapeless; history is a way of lending shape to the past by focusing on significant events and their relationships. Your "history" of last night's dinner will include only the significant elements, perhaps who your companions were and why you got together, not where the spinach was grown.

Second, the historical record is limited. As you will discover, there is much we don't know about everyday life in seventeenth-century America. History must be based on fact and evidence. The historian then, using the evidence available, fashions a story in which certain past events are connected and take on special meaning or significance. If we accept this definition, we will recognize that much history is subjective, or influenced by the perspective and bias of the historian attempting to give meaning to events.

This is why there is so much disagreement about the importance of some past events. You may have been taught in high school that it was important simply to learn dates and facts: that the Declaration of Independence was adopted on July 4, 1776, or that Franklin Roosevelt was inaugurated on March 4, 1933. But these facts by themselves are limited in meaning. They gain significance when they become parts of larger stories, such as why the American colonies revolted against England, or how America responded to the Great Depression. When historians construct stories or narratives in which these facts or events take on special significance, room for disagreement creeps in.

Since it is valid for historians to disagree, you should not automatically accept what any one historian writes. You should learn to apply general rules of logic and evidence in assessing the validity of different historical interpretations. This *Study Guide* will at times give you an opportunity to assess different interpretations of events. By doing this you will learn to question what you read and hear, to think critically.

HOW TO READ A TEXTBOOK

Reading a textbook should be both pleasurable and profitable. The responsibility for this is partly the author's and partly yours, the reader's. George Tindall has written a text which should teach and entertain. In order to get the most out of it you must read actively and critically. One way to avoid passive, mindless reading is to write, underline, or highlight material by hand. Thus simply by highlighting or underlining pertinent passages in the textbook you will later be better able to recall what you have read and you will be able to review quickly important material. The key to effective highlighting is to be judicious about what you choose to mark. You should highlight key words and phrases, not whole sentences unless all the words are important. For example, the two paragraphs below from Chapter 2 of the textbook (pp. 43–44) show the way I would highlight them:

Even the Tudors, who acted as autocrats, preserved the forms of constitutional procedure. In the making of laws the king's subjects consented through representatives in the House of Commons. By custom and practice **the principle was established that the king taxed his subjects only with the consent of Parliament.** And by its control of the purse strings Parliament would draw other strands of power into its hands. This structure of habit broadened down from precedent to precedent to form a **constitution that was** not written in one place, or for that matter, **not fully written down at all.** The *Magna Charta* of 1215, for instance, had been a statement of privileges wrested by certain nobles from the king, but it became part of a broader tradition that the people as a whole had rights which even the king could not violate.

A further buttress to English liberty was the **great body of common law** which had developed since the twelfth century in royal courts established to check the arbitrary caprice of local nobles. Without laws to cover every detail, judges had to exercise their own ideas of fairness in settling disputes. **Decisions once made became precedents for later decisions** and over the years a body of judge-made law developed, the outgrowth more of experience than of abstract logic. Through the courts the principle evolved that **a subject could be arrested or his goods seized only upon a warrant issued by a court** and that **he was entitled to a trial by a jury of his peers** (his equals) in accordance with established rules of evidence.

Probably no two persons would agree on exactly what words in the passage should be underlined, but you can readily see that I have emphasized only the major points concerning English justice.

Highlighting like this can be helpful, but even more useful in increasing your retention of the material is to jot down brief notes about what you read. For example, from the passage above you might list some key elements in the development of liberty under the Tudors: the principle that the king could tax his subjects only with the consent of Parliament, the development of an unwritten constitution, the principle that a court order was required for arrest or seizure of property, and the principle of trial by jury.

Taking notes makes it easier to commit important points to memory. This will help especially when you review for a test.

ACKNOWLEDGMENTS

The work on this *Study Guide* would not have been possible without the assistance of a number of people. The many years of inspiration from George B. Tindall have contributed immeasurably to my professional growth. The positive features this work has for students and instructors stem from his suggestions as well as from my teaching experience at Winthrop College and other institutions. In the course of writing this *Study Guide* I have learned the value of a good editor. Steve Forman's critical suggestions, generous support, and constant prodding contributed greatly to the final product. Assistance in typing and many other details was generously given by Jean Morse, secretary to the Department of History and Geography at Winthrop College. Birdsall Viault, chairman of that department, was also generous with his support and encouragement. Critical comments from two student readers of the initial chapters, Scot Heavner and Kelly Bristow, helped me to get the work on the right track. My student assistant, Deborah Shropshire, has contributed highly competent research in checking documents and readings. As always, my wife Nancy has been by best editorial critic and a continuing source of encouragement. My sons Kevin, Christopher, and David cheerfully tolerated the near-loss of a father's companionship for a number of months.

T.S.M.

18

RECONSTRUCTION: NORTH AND SOUTH

CHAPTER OBJECTIVES

After you complete the reading and study of this chapter, you should be able to

1. Describe the impact of the Civil War on both the South and the North and on the status of freed blacks.
2. Explain the circumstances which led to Radical Reconstruction.
3. Describe the nature and extent of Radical Reconstruction.
4. Explain the process which returned control of the South to the conservatives.
5. Evaluate the contributions and failures of the Grant administration.
6. Explain the outcome of the election of 1876 and the effects of that election and the special arrangements made to conclude it.
7. Evaluate the overall impact of Reconstruction.

CHAPTER OUTLINE

I. Impact of the Civil War
   A. Casualties greater than any war before World War II
   B. Nationalism triumphant
   C. Abolition of slavery
   D. A social revolution
   E. Northern congressional enactments during the Civil War
   F. Devastation in the South
      1. Physical devastation
      2. Property values collapsed
      3. Loss of slaves
   G. Status of freed blacks
      1. Lack of resources
      2. Congress hesitant to distribute land
      3. Confiscation of southern lands
      4. Work of the Freedmen's Bureau

II. Development of a plan of Reconstruction
   A. Loyal counties of Virginia
   B. Military governors in Tennessee, Arkansas, and Louisiana
   C. Lincoln's plan of Reconstruction
      1. Provisions
      2. Implementation in Tennessee, Arkansas, and Louisiana
      3. Congressional reaction
      4. Counterclaims of Lincoln and Congress
      5. Wade-Davis Bill
      6. Lincoln's response to the Wade-Davis Bill
      7. Lincoln's final statement on Reconstruction

III. The assassination of Lincoln

IV. Andrew Johnson and Reconstruction
   A. Johnson's background
   B. Radicals' perception of him

C. Johnson's plan for Reconstruction
D. End of land redistribution

V. Southern state reorganization
   A. Actions taken
   B. Southern intransigence
   C. Congressional reaction to southern states
   D. Provisions and impact of Black Codes

VI. The Radicals
   A. Joint Committee on Reconstruction
   B. Radical motivation
   C. Constitutional theories of status of southern states

VII. Johnson and Congress in battle
   A. Veto of Freedman's Bureau extension
   B. Effect of Johnson's Washington's Birthday speech
   C. Congress overrides veto of the Civil Rights Act
   D. The Fourteenth Amendment
   E. Race riots in the South
   F. The congressional elections

VIII. Congressional Reconstruction triumphant
   A. Actions in Congress early in 1867
      1. Extension of suffrage in District of Columbia
      2. Requirement that new Congress convene
      3. Command of the Army Act
      4. Tenure of Office Act
      5. Military Reconstruction Act
         a. Key provisions for black suffrage and the Fourteenth Amendment
         b. Tennessee exempted
         c. Military districts
   B. Later Reconstruction Acts to plug loopholes

IX. Constitutional issues and the Supreme Court
   A. *Ex Parte Milligan* strikes down a wartime court-martial conviction
   B. *Cummings v. Missouri* and *Ex Parte Garland* overrule laws antagonistic to ex-Confederates
   C. Congress removes right of Congress to decide *Ex Parte McCardle*
   D. *Texas v. White* upheld Congressional Reconstruction

X. The impeachment and trial of Johnson
   A. Failure of early efforts to impeach him
   B. Violation of Tenure of Office Act
   C. The articles of impeachment
   D. The Senate trial
   E. Ramifications of the impeachment

XI. Radical rule in the South
   A. Readmission of southern states
   B. Duration of Radical control
   C. Role of the Union League prior to Reconstruction
   D. Blacks in southern politics
      1. Characteristics of black control
      2. Extent of black control
   E. Carpetbaggers and scalawags
   F. Nature of new state constitutions

XII. Achievements of the Radical governments

XIII. The measure of corruption and abuse
   A. Examples of abuse in Radical governments
   B. Examples of abuse in other parts of the nation

XIV. The development of white terror techniques
   A. Objections to black participation in government
   B. The Ku Klux Klan
   C. Enforcement Acts to protect black voters

XV. The return of conservative control
   A. Reasons for abandonment of the Radical programs
   B. Duration of Radical control

XVI. The Grant years
   A. The election of 1868
      1. Reasons for support of Grant
      2. The Grant ticket and platform
      3. Democratic programs and candidates
      4. Results
   B. The character of Grant's leadership
   C. Early appointments
   D. Proposal to pay the government debt
   E. Reform and the election of 1872
      1. Liberal Republicans nominate Greeley in 1872
      2. Grant's advantages
   F. Scandals
      1. Jay Gould's effort to corner the gold market

2. The Crédit Mobilier exposure
3. Belknap and the Indian Bureau
4. Other scandals
5. Grant's personal role in the
   scandals
G. Economic panic
   1. Causes for the depression
   2. Severity of the depression
H. Democratic control of the House in
   1874
I. Reissue of greenbacks
J. Resumption of specie payments
   approved in 1875

XVII. Election of 1876
   A. Elimination of Grant and Blaine

B. Republicans nominate Hayes
C. Democrats nominate Tilden
D. Views of the parties
E. Results of the popular vote
F. Creation of the Electoral
   Commission
   1. Stacked for Tilden
   2. Restacked for Hayes
   3. Its report
G. Wormley House bargain
   1. Promises of each side
   2. Promises filled and unfilled
H. The end of Reconstruction
   1. A betrayal of the blacks?
   2. An enduring legacy

KEY ITEMS OF CHRONOLOGY

Lincoln's plan for Reconstruction announced	1863
Creation of Freedmen's Bureau	1865
Assassination of Lincoln	April 14, 1865
Johnson's plan for Reconstruction announced	May 29, 1865
Veto of Freedmen's Bureau Extension Bill	February 1866
Congress overrode Johnson's veto of Civil Rights Bill	April 1866
Ku Klux Klan organized in the South	1866
Military Reconstruction Act	March 2, 1867
Johnson replaced Stanton with Grant as secretary of war	August 1867
Johnson named Thomas secretary of war	February 1868
House voted to impeach Johnson	February 1868
Trial of Johnson in Senate	March 5 to May 26, 1868
All southern states except Virginia, Mississippi, and Texas readmitted to Congress	June 1868
Mississippi, Texas, and Virginia readmitted	1870
Texas v. White decision of Supreme Court	1869
Grant administrations	1869–1877
Thirteenth Amendment ratified	1865
Fourteenth Amendment ratified	1868
Fifteenth Amendment ratified	1870
Resumption Act	1875

TERMS TO MASTER

Listed below are some important terms or people with which you should be familiar *after you complete the study of this chapter. Identify each name or term.*

1. Freedmen's Bureau
2. Lincoln's plan for Reconstruction

3. Wade-Davis Bill
4. Johnson's Proclamation of Amnesty
5. Black Codes
6. Radicals
7. Fourteenth Amendment
8. Military Reconstruction
9. Command of the Army Act
10. Tenure of Office Act
11. *Ex Parte McCardle*
12. carpetbaggers
13. scalawags
14. Ku Klux Klan
15. "Ohio Idea"
16. Liberal Republicans
17. Jay Gould
18. Crédit Mobilier
19. Samuel J. Tilden
20. Compromise of 1877

VOCABULARY BUILDING

Listed below are some words or phrases used in this chapter. Look in the dictionary for the meaning of each term not defined here for you.

1. bushwhackers
2. shibboleths
3. aegis
4. cajoled

EXERCISES FOR UNDERSTANDING

When you have completed the reading of the chapter, answer each of the following questions. If you have difficulty, go back to the text and reread the section of the chapter related to the question.

Multiple-Choice Questions

Select the letter of the response which best completes the statement.

1. What was the greatest unfulfilled need of freed blacks in 1865?
   A. formal action to outlaw slavery
   B. the right to work on their former plantations

C. land of their own
D. the right to marry legally

2. Lincoln's plan for Reconstruction called for
   A. permitting officers of the Confederacy to continue to exercise rights of citizenship
   B. the right to form a new state government as soon as a number equal to 10 percent of the state's 1860 voters had sworn allegiance to the United States
   C. a requirement that the only southerners who could vote were those who had *not* supported the Confederacy
   D. forty acres of free land to be given to all freed slaves

3. The Black Codes were
   A. regulations of the Freedmen's Bureau to protect freed slaves
   B. laws passed by black-dominated southern legislatures
   C. a system of secret communication to be used by ex-slaves.
   D. southern state laws which restricted the rights of freed blacks

4. Johnson's plan of Reconstruction differed from Lincoln's primarily in providing
   A. that states had to have a majority of the people take an oath of allegiance to the United States before they could organize
   B. for an ironclad oath from all persons who wished to vote
   C. that all property holders of $20,000 in value were to be banned from receiving automatic pardons and forced to appeal directly to the president for a pardon
   D. full voting rights for blacks

5. The constitutional view of southern state status which prevailed in Congress was
   A. the "state suicide" theory
   B. the "conquered provinces" view
   C. acceptance of the reality of secession
   D. the "forfeited rights" theory

6. Johnson was impeached for
   A. embezzling federal funds
   B. refusing to obey the Tenure of Office Act

C. refusing to turn documents over to Congress for their investigation

D. all of the above

7. The Fourteenth Amendment provided that state representation in Congress could be reduced for
   A. failure to free blacks from slavery
   B. refusal to allow black adult males to vote
   C. refusing the right to vote to any citizen
   D. not ratifying the Fourteenth Amendment

8. U.S. Grant was guilty of
   A. refusing to turn documents over to Congress for their investigation
   B. trying to block the implementation of Reconstruction laws
   C. choosing his appointees unwisely
   D. taking funds from the federal treasury

True-False Questions

Indicate whether each statement is true or false.

1. The Radicals' first reaction to Andrew Johnson as president was favorable because they thought he would be harsher on the South than Lincoln had been.

2. In the election of 1866 Johnson's Union party gained votes in Congress.

3. The Congress refused to allow the Supreme Court to review the case of *Ex Parte McCardle.*

4. At his impeachment, Johnson failed to be convicted by one vote in the Senate.

5. All southern states had been readmitted to the Union by the end of 1870.

6. Blacks dominated the legislatures in five southern states.

7. Corruption in government was not confined to the South in the Reconstruction era.

8. Grant as president sought to encourage inflation through the issuing of more greenbacks by the federal government.

Essay Questions

1. Discuss the impact of the Civil War on the South, the North, and the slaves.

2. In what ways was the Freedmen's Bureau expected to help blacks in the South? To what degree was it successful? Explain.

3. Explain how and why Johnson's plan of Reconstruction failed.

4. Radical Reconstruction was not imposed until two years after the end of the Civil War and caused bitter opposition from the whites in the South. Would it have been better accepted if it had been imposed in May 1865 instead of March 1867? Explain why or why not.

5. Review the terms of the Thirteenth, Fourteenth, and Fifteenth Amendments and determine which had the greatest impact on the United States.

6. What benefits were brought to the South during Radical rule?

7. Account for the scandals of the Grant administrations. Are these the only lasting developments his administration should be known for? Explain.

8. Which side won the most in the Compromise of 1877? Explain.

READINGS

Reading 1. Claude Bowers Sees Venal Radicals Torturing the South

Like other significant periods in American history, the Reconstruction Era has gone through cycles of interpretation. Some of the earliest scholarly work on the period was carried out by William A. Dunning and his students, who believed that the Radicals sought to impose their rule on the South for selfish motives of personal gain. Later revisionists have considerably altered that view. The passage below comes from a popular account of Reconstruction written in 1929. It presents the negative image of Radical motives and accomplishments.

If Hilaire Belloc is right in his opinion that "readable history is melodrama," the true story of the twelve tragic years that followed the death of Lincoln should be entertaining. They were years of revolutionary turmoil, with the elemental passions predominant, and with broken bones and bloody noses among the fighting factionalists. The prevailing note was one of tragedy, though, as we shall see, there was an abundance of comedy, and not a little of farce. Never have American public men in responsible positions, directing the destiny of the Nation, been so brutal, hypocritical, and corrupt. The Constitution was treated as a doormat on which politicians and army officers wiped their feet after wading in the muck. Never has the Supreme Court been treated with such ineffable contempt, and never has that tribunal so often cringed before the clamor of the mob.

So appalling is the picture of these revolutionary years that even historians have preferred to overlook many essential things. Thus, Andrew Johnson, who fought the bravest battle for constitutional liberty and for the preservation of our institutions ever waged by an Executive, until recently was left in the pillory to which unscrupulous gamblers for power consigned him, because the unvarnished truth that vindicates him makes so many statues in public squares and parks seem a bit grotesque. That Johnson was maligned by his enemies because he was seeking honestly to carry out the conciliatory and wise policy of Lincoln is now generally understood, but even now few realize how intensely Lincoln was hated by the Radicals at the time of his death.

A complete understanding of this period calls for a reappraisal of many public men. Some statesmen we have been taught to reverence will appear in these pages in sorry rôles. Others, who played conspicuous parts, but have been denied the historical recognition due them, are introduced and shown in action. Thus the able leaders of the minority in Congress are given fuller treatment than has been fashionable, since they represented more Americans. Others, who played conspicuous parts, but have been denied the historical recognition due them, are introduced and shown in action. Thus the able leaders of the minority in Congress are given fuller treatment than has been fashionable, since they represented more Americans, North and South, than the leaders of the Radical majority, and were nearer right on the issues of reconstruction. Thus, too, the brilliant and colorful leaders and spokesmen of the South are given their proper place in the dramatic struggle for the preservation of Southern civilization and the redemption of their people. I have sought to re-create the black and bloody drama of these years, to show the leaders of the fighting factions at close range, to picture the moving masses, both whites and blacks, in North and South, surging crazily under the influence of the poisonous propaganda on which they were fed.

That the Southern people literally were put to the torture is vaguely understood, but even historians have shrunk from the un-happy task of showing us the torture chambers. It is impossible to grasp the real significance of the revolutionary proceedings of the rugged conspirators working out the policies of Thaddeus Stevens without making many journeys among the Southern people, and seeing with our own eyes the indignities to which they were subjected. Through many unpublished contemporary family letters and diaries, I have tried to show the psychological effect upon them of the despotic policies of which they were the victims. Brutal men, inspired by personal ambition or party motives, as-sumed the pose of philanthropists and patriots, and thus deceived and misguided vast numbers of well-meaning people in the North.

[From Claude G. Bowers, *The Tragic Era: The Revolution after Lincoln* (New York: Blue Ribbon Books, 1929), pp. v–vi]

Reading 2. William A. Dunning Explains the Failure of Reconstruction

William A. Dunning, a historian at Columbia University around the turn of the century, wrote a synthesis of Reconstruction from a southern point of view and directed a school of scholars who investigated developments in states in the South from a , similar viewpoint. In these excerpts Dunning, while explaining the failure of Reconstruction, reveals his attitude about the corruption and inadequacy of Reconstruction governments and his reservations about race. What insights do you find in his views?

The leading motive of the reconstruction had been, at the inception of the process, to insure to the freedmen an effective protection of their civil rights,—of life, liberty, and property. In the course of the process, the chief stress came to be laid on the endowment of the blacks with full political rights,—with the electoral franchise and eligibility to office. And by the time the process was complete, a very important, if not the most important part had been played by the desire and the purpose to secure to the Republican party the permanent control of several Southern states in which hitherto such a political organization had been unknown. This last motive had a plausible and widely accepted justification in the view that the rights of the negro and the "results of the war" in general would be secure only if the national government should remain indefinitely in Republican hands, and that therefore the strengthening of the party was a primary dictate of patriotism.

Through the operation of these various motives successive and simultaneous, the completion of the reconstruction showed the fol-lowing situation: (1) the negroes were in the enjoyment of the equal political rights with the whites; (2) the Republican party was in vigorous life in all the Southern states, and in firm control of many of them; and (3) the negroes exercised an influence in political affairs out of all relation to their intelligence or property, and, since so many of the whites were defranchised, excessive even in propor-tion to their numbers. At the present day, in the same states, the negroes enjoy practically no political rights; the Republican party is but the shadow of a name; and the influence of the negroes in political affairs is nil. This contrast suggests what has been involved in the undoing of reconstruction.

Before the last state was restored to the Union the process was well under way through which the resumption of control by the whites was to be effected. The tendency in this direction was greatly promoted by conditions within the Republican party itself. Two years of supremacy in those states which had been restored in 1868 had revealed unmistakable evidences of moral and political weakness in the governments. The personnel of the party was declining in character through the return to the North of the more substantial of the carpet-baggers, who found Southern conditions, both social and industrial, far from what they had anticipated, and through the very frequent instances in which the "scalawags" ran to open disgrace. Along with this deterioration in the white element of the party, the negroes who rose to prominence and leadership were very frequently of a type which acquired and practiced the tricks and knavery rather than the useful arts of politics, and the vicious courses of these negroes strongly confirmed the prejudices of the whites. But at the same time that the incapacity of the party in power to administer any government was becoming demonstrable the problems with which it was required to cope were made by its adversaries such as would have taxed the capacity of the most efficient statesmen the world could produce. . . . No attention was paid to the claim that the manifest inefficiency and viciousness of the Republican governments afforded a partial, if not wholly adequate explanation of their overthrow. Not even the relative quiet and order that followed the triumph of the whites in these states were recognized as justifying the new regime. [From William A. Dunning, "The Undoing of Reconstruction," in *The Atlantic Monthly*, 88 (October 1901), pp. 437–438.]

Reading 3. Eric Foner Contends That Reconstruction Did Not Go Far Enough

Historical scholarship on the Reconstruction era continues to grow at a remarkable rate. In the following excerpt

Eric Foner summarizes some of the most recent scholarship and suggests a new way to view Reconstruction.

Despite the excellence of recent writing and the continual expansion of our knowledge of the period, historians of Reconstruction today face a unique dilemma. An old interpretation has been overthrown, but a coherent new synthesis has yet to take its place. The revisionists of the 1960s effectively established a series of negative points: the Reconstruction governments were not as bad as had been portrayed, black supremacy was a myth, the Radicals were not cynical manipulators of the freedmen. Yet no convincing overall portrait of the quality of political and social life emerged from their writings.

. . . a new portrait of Reconstruction ought to begin by viewing it not as a specific time period, bounded by the years 1865 and 1877, but as an episode in a prolonged historical process—American society's adjustment to the consequences of the Civil War and emancipation.

> . . . the focal point of Reconstruction was the social revolution known as emancipation. Plantation slavery was simultaneously a system of labor, a form of racial domination, and the foundation upon which arose a distinctive ruling class within the South. Its demise threw open the most fundamental questions of economy, society, and politics. A new system of labor, social, racial, and political relations had to be created to replace slavery.

Few modern scholars believe the Reconstruction governments established in the South in 1867 and 1868 fulfilled the aspirations of their humble constituents. While their achievements in such realms as education, civil rights, and the economic rebuilding of the South are now widely appreciated, historians today believe they failed to affect either the economic plight of the emancipated slave or the ongoing transformation of independent white farmers into cotton tenants. Yet their opponents did perceive the Reconstruction governments in precisely this way—as representatives of a revolution that had put the bottom rail, both racial and economic, on top. This perception helps explain the ferocity of the attacks leveled against them and the pervasiveness of violence in the postemancipation South.

The spectacle of black men voting and holding office was anathema to large numbers of Southern whites. Even more disturbing, at least in the view of those who still controlled the plantation regions of the South, was the emergence of local officials, black and white, who sympathized with the plight of the black laborer. . . . During presidential Reconstruction, and after "Redemption," with planters and their allies in control of politics, the law emerged as a means of stabilizing and promoting the plantation system. If Radical Reconstruction failed to redistribute the land of the South, the ouster of the planter class from control of politics at least ensured that the sanctions of the criminal law would not be employed to discipline the black labor force.

An understanding of this fundamental conflict over the relation between government and society helps explain the pervasive complaints concerning corruption and "extravagance" during Radical Reconstruction. Corruption there was aplenty; tax rates did rise sharply. More significant than the rate of taxation, however, was the change in its incidence. For the first time, planters and white farmers had to pay a significant portion of their income to the government, while propertyless blacks often escaped scot-free. Several states, moreover, enacted heavy taxes on uncultivated land to discourage land speculation and force land onto the market, benefiting, it was hoped, the freedmen.

As time passed, complaints about the "extravagance" and corruption of Southern governments found a sympathetic audience among influential Northerners. The Democratic charge that universal suffrage in the South was responsible for high taxes and governmental extravagance coincided with a rising conviction among the urban middle classes of the North that city government had to be taken out of the hands of the immigrant poor and returned to the "best men"—the educated, professional, financially independent citizens unable to exert much political influence at a time of mass parties and machine politics. Increasingly the "respectable" middle classes began to retreat from the very notion of universal suffrage. The poor were no longer perceived as honest producers, the backbone of the social order; now they became the "dangerous classes," the "mob." As the historian Francis Parkman put it, too much power rested with "masses of imported ignorance and hereditary ineptitude." To Parkman the Irish of the Northern cities and the blacks of the South were equally incapable of utilizing the ballot: "Witness the municipal corruptions of New York, and the monstrosities of negro rule in South Carolina." Such attitudes helped to justify Northern inaction as, one by one, the Reconstruction regimes of the South were overthrown by political violence.

In the end, then, neither the abolition of slavery nor Reconstruction succeeded in resolving the debate over the meaning of freedom in American life. Twenty years before the American Civil War, writing about the prospect of abolition in France's colonies, Alexis de Tocqueville had written, "If the Negroes have the right to become free, the [planters] have the incontestable right not to be ruined by the Negroes' freedom." And in the United States, as in nearly every plantation society that experienced the end of slavery, a rigid social and political dichotomy between former master and former slave, an ideology of racism, and a dependent labor force with limited economic opportunities all survived abolition. Unless one means by freedom the simple fact of not being a slave, emancipation thrust blacks into a kind of no-man's land, a partial freedom that made a mockery of the American ideal of equal citizenship.

Yet by the same token the ultimate outcome underscores the uniqueness of Reconstruction itself. Alone among the societies that abolished slavery in the nineteenth century, the United States, for a moment, offered the freedmen a measure of political control over their own destinies. However brief its sway, Reconstruction allowed scope for a remarkable political and social mobilization of the black community. It opened doors of opportunity that could never be completely closed. Reconstruction transformed the lives of Southern blacks in ways unmeasurable by statistics and unreachable by law. It raised their expectations and aspirations, redefined their status in relation to the larger society, and allowed space for the creation of institutions that enabled them to survive the repression that followed. And it established constitutional principles of civil and political equality that, while flagrantly violated after Redemption, planted the seeds of future struggle.

[From Eric Foner, "The New View of Reconstruction," in *American Heritage* 34, no. 6 (October-November 1983): 13–15]

Questions for Reflection

What evidence is there in the first two readings to show that Dunning found Reconstruction less despicable a development than Bowers did? What good does Dunning seem to imply came from Reconstruction? Select some of the words and phrases which Bowers used to give an emotional tone to his account. Is Dunning more convincing to the reader? What appear to be Dunning's views on race?

What does Dunning mean by "The failure of Radicalism is thus a part of the wider failure of bourgeois liberalism to solve the problems of the new age which was dawning"?

According to Eric Foner, how did Reconstruction lead to the ouster of the planter class from control of politics and why was that important? How did attitudes toward blacks in Reconstruction interact with attitudes toward immigrants and other oppressed groups in the North? Why does Foner think that Reconstruction did not succeed in giving blacks freedom?

All three passages find a failure in Reconstruction from one perspective or another. How do you think the problems of Reconstruction of the South could have been better solved?

ANSWERS TO MULTIPLE-CHOICE AND TRUE-FALSE QUESTIONS

Multiple-Choice Questions

1-C, 2-B, 3-D, 4-C, 5-D, 6-B, 7-B, 8-C

True-False Questions

1-T, 2-F, 3-T, 4-T, 5-T, 6-F, 7-T, 8-F

19

NEW FRONTIERS: SOUTH AND WEST

CHAPTER OBJECTIVES

After you complete the reading and study of this chapter, you should be able to:

1. Explain the concept of the New South, its development, and how it affected the South after the Civil War.
2. Account for the rise of the Bourbons to power in the South and explain their impact on the South.
3. Explain the causes and process of disfranchisement of blacks in the South.
4. Compare the views of Washington and Du Bois on the place of blacks in American life.
5. Describe the Indian wars and explain the new Indian policy of 1887.
6. Describe the rise and decline of the cattle industry.
7. Describe the problems of farming on the western frontier.
8. Explain the importance of Turner's theory of the significance of the frontier in American history.

CHAPTER OUTLINE

I. The New South
   A. Concept of the New South
      1. Henry Grady's background
      2. His vision
      3. Other prophets of the New South Creed
      4. Industrial fairs: Atlanta International Cotton Exposition of 1881
   B. Economic growth
      1. Growth of cotton textile manufacturing
      2. Development of the tobacco industry
         a. John Ruffin Green and Bull's Head
         b. Duke family
         c. Techniques used by Buck Duke for growth
         d. Creation and breakup of the American Tobacco Company
      3. Coal production
      4. Lumbering
      5. Other products
         a. Phosphate fertilizers
         b. Canned oysters, vegetables, and fruits
         c. Shipbuilding
         d. Leather products
         e. Wagons and buggies
         f. Liquors and beverages
         g. Paper, clay, glass, and stone products
         h. Beginnings of petroleum and hydroelectric power
   C. Agriculture in the New South

1. Limited diversity in agriculture
2. Features of sharecropping and tenancy
3. Impact of the crop lien system
D. Role of the Bourbon Redeemers
  1. Nature of the Bourbons
  2. Bourbon economic policies
    a. Laissez-faire
    b. Retrenchment in government spending
    c. Assistance of private philanthropy
    d. Convict lease system
    e. Repudiation of Confederate debts in some states
    f. Positive contributions of the Bourbons
E. Role of the Democratic party in the New South
  1. Nature of the mongrel coalition
  2. Basis for independent political movements
  3. Efforts for Republican and independent collaboration
F. Disfranchisement of blacks
  1. Bourbon-black compatibility in politics
  2. Varied development of color lines in social relations
  3. Impetus for elimination of the black vote
  4. Techniques used to exclude blacks
  5. Spread of segregation
    a. Use on railway cars
    b. Impact of Civil Rights Cases, 1883
    c. Impact of *Plessy v. Ferguson*, 1896
    d. Spread of segregation
  6. Spread of violence against blacks
G. Clash of Booker T. Washington and W. E. B. Du Bois
H. Role of myth in the New South
  1. Lack of distinctiveness in the Bourbon-Redeemer Era
  2. Curious linkage of Old and New South
  3. Benefits of linking the New South with the Old
  4. The ultimate achievement of the New South prophets

II. The New West
A. Nature of the West after the War

B. Environment beyond 98° West longitude
C. Developments which altered the Great American Desert
D. The mining frontier
  1. Pattern of mining development
  2. Locations of major mineral discoveries
  3. Development of new states
E. Displacement of the Indians
  1. Agreement for tribal limitations, 1851
  2. Conflicts which arose during the Civil War
  3. Establishment of Indian Peace Commission, 1867
    a. Policy of two large reservations
    b. Agreements with the Indians in 1867 and 1868
  4. Continued resistance of Indians
    a. Massacre at Little Big Horn
    b. Conquest of Sioux and others
    c. Significance of Chief Joseph and Nez Perce
    d. Ghost Dance movement
  5. Impact of annihilation of buffalo herds
  6. Stirrings for reform in Indian policy
    a. Eastern view of Indian slaughter
    b. Role of Helen Hunt Jackson
  7. Dawes Severalty Act, 1887
    a. Concept of new policy
    b. Provisions of Dawes and subsequent acts
    c. Impact of new policy
F. The cattle industry in the West
  1. Development of the open range
  2. War's increased demand for beef
  3. Renewal of long drives after the Civil War
    a. Joseph McCoy
    b. Features of the cowtown
  4. Codes of the open range
  5. Boom and bust in the open range
    a. Causes for boom
    b. Causes for decline of the open range
    c. Romance of the cowboy
G. The farming frontier
  1. Land policy after the Civil War
  2. Changed institutions beyond the 100th meridian
  3. Efforts for reclamation of arid lands

4. An assessment of land distribution
5. Aspects of farming and life on the Great Plains
6. New farming implements
   a. Bonanza farms

b. Small farms
H. Turner's frontier thesis
   1. Turner's claims for the frontier
   2. Other views

KEY ITEMS OF CHRONOLOGY

Homestead Act	1862
First of the long drives	1866
Indian Peace Commission settlements	1867–1868
Civil Rights Cases	1883
Dawes Severalty Act	1887
Mississippi Constitution incorporates disfranchisement of blacks	1890
Census shows frontier closed	1890
Turner frontier thesis presented	1893
Plessy v. Ferguson	1896
Disfranchisement of blacks essentially completed in southern states	1910

TERMS TO MASTER

Listed below are some important terms or people with which you should be familiar after you complete the study of this chapter. Explain the significance of each name or term.

1. Henry Woodfin Grady
2. James Buchanan Duke
3. sharecropping
4. crop lien system
5. Bourbons
6. Peabody Fund for Education
7. Readjuster party
8. Mississippi Plan for disfranchisement
9. grandfather clauses
10. Civil Rights Cases
11. *Plessy v. Ferguson*
12. Booker T. Washington
13. W. E. B. Du Bois
14. Great American Desert
15. Indian Peace Commission
16. Chief Joseph
17. Wovoka
18. Helen Hunt Jackson
19. Dawes Severalty Act
20. long drives
21. "dry farming"
22. Frederick Jackson Turner

VOCABULARY BUILDING

Listed below are some words or phrases used in this chapter. Look up each word in your dictionary unless the meaning is given here.

1. harbinger
2. ubiquitous
3. cotery
4. epithet
5. eschew
6. parsimony
7. escutcheon
8. parsimonious
9. heterodox
10. finesse
11. octoroon
12. pernicious
13. hauteur
14. brahmin (Boston brahmin)
15. accouterments
16. sourdough

17. hiatus
18. endemic
19. myrmidons
20. bushwhackers
21. bovine and ovine species
22. hegemony
23. rigmarole

EXERCISES FOR UNDERSTANDING

When you have completed the reading of the chapter, answer each of the following questions. If you have difficulty, go back and reread the section of the chapter related to the question.

Multiple-Choice Questions

Select the letter of the response which best completes the statement.

1. Henry Grady's concept of the New South placed greatest emphasis on
   A. diversifying agriculture
   B. achieving equality for blacks
   C. more democratic political procedures
   D. development of industry

2. James B. Duke's greatest contribution to the South's progress was in
   A. development of the cigarette industry
   B. promotion of education
   C. development of new inventions
   D. seeking to achieve greater competition among various companies in all industries in the South

3. The most significant impact of the crop lien system in the South was that it
   A. made possible cash payments for goods
   B. provided a source of labor in the post-Reconstruction South
   C. made possible low-interest-rate loans for blacks
   D. encouraged keeping the South on the one crop, cotton

4. Bourbon policies included *all but which one* of the following?
   A. reduction of expenditures for education
   B. increased funds for prisons
   C. efforts to regulate railroad rates
   D. development of state colleges for Negroes

5. The settlement of the Great Plains beyond 98° West was encouraged because
   A. a cycle of rain after 1871 suggested that the climate of the area was changing
   B. of the excellent free lands provided by the Homestead Act
   C. of the development of barbed wire
   D. of all of the above

6. The Indian policy developed by the Dawes Act provided for
   A. free land for all Indians
   B. eventual citizenship for Indians
   C. breakup of all Indian reservations
   D. all of the above

7. Open-range cattle raising ended because
   A. farmers fenced off their lands
   B. sheep herding grew and the sheep began to graze on the same land the cattle did
   C. the severe winters of 1886 and 1887 hurt the cattle
   D. of all of the above

8. Turner claimed that the frontier gave the United States
   A. its wealth and diversity
   B. a strong sense of individualism
   C. idealism as opposed to practicality
   D. all of the above

True-False Questions

Indicate whether each statement is true or false.

1. The first expansion of industry sought by the South was in cotton textiles.
2. Among the industries developed by James B. Duke was hydroelectric power.
3. The Democratic party managed to exclude blacks from voting with the all-white primary.
4. The Mississippi Plan included the grandfather clause which excluded all persons whose fathers were slaves.
5. The *Plessy v. Ferguson* decision included

a ruling that states could not interfere with the rights of blacks.

6. The linkage of Henry Grady with Joel Chandler Harris in the Atlanta *Constitution* was an example of the Bourbon paradox.

7. The Ghost Dance movement was an effort of the Indians to demonstrate a new sense of identity in their continuing clash with white culture.

Essay Questions

1. What was Henry Grady's vision for the New South? What changes did it represent from the Old South?

2. Describe the economic growth that was evident in the South after Reconstruction.

3. What role was played by the Bourbon Redeemers in the South? To what extent did they really "redeem" the South?

4. Describe the process by which the blacks were disfranchised in the late nineteenth century. How was this action justified by the whites?

5. Contrast the vision which Booker T. Washington and W. E. B. Du Bois had for freed blacks. Whose ideas do you think were sounder?

6. How did United States policy toward the Indians change from 1865 to 1887? Why did it change?

7. How did land policy encourage westward movement after the Civil War?

8. What area had more potential for progress in the late nineteenth century: the South or the West? Explain.

DOCUMENTS

Document 1. Booker T. Washington Proposes the "Atlanta Compromise"

Invited to appear before a national audience at the Atlanta Exposition in 1895, Booker T. Washington carefully honed a speech asserting the importance of the black contribution to America and the South, but without offending white sensibilities. The speech was widely acclaimed among whites and blacks alike.

One-third of the population of the South is of the Negro race. No enterprise seeking the material, civil, or moral welfare of this section can disregard this element of our population and reach the highest success. . . .

Ignorant and inexperienced, it is not strange that in the first years of our new life we began at the top instead of at the bottom; that a seat in Congress or the state legislature was more sought than real estate or industrial skill; that the political convention or stump speaking had more attractions than starting a dairy farm or truck garden.

A ship lost at sea for many days suddenly sighted a friendly vessel. From the mast of the unfortunate vessel was seen a signal, "Water, water; we die of thirst!" The answer from the friendly vessel at once came back, "Cast down your bucket where you are." A second time the signal, "Water, water; send us water!" ran up from the distressed vessel, and was answered, "Cast down your bucket where you are." The captain of the distressed vessel, at last heeding the injunction, cast down his bucket, and it came up full of fresh, sparkling water from the mouth of the Amazon River. To those of my race who depend on bettering their condition in a foreign land or who underestimate the importance of cultivating friendly relations with the Southern white man, who is their next-door neighbour, I would say: "Cast down your bucket where you are"—cast it down in making friends in every manly way of the people of all races by whom we are surrounded.

Cast it down in agriculture, mechanics, in commerce, in domestic service, and in the professions. And in this connection it is well to bear in mind that whatever other sins the South may be called to bear, when it comes to business, pure and simple, it is in the South that the Negro is given a man's chance in the commercial world, and in nothing is this Exposition more eloquent than in emphasizing this chance. Our greatest danger is that in the great leap from slavery to freedom we may overlook the fact that the masses of us are to live by the productions of our hands, and fail to keep in mind that we shall prosper in proportion as we learn to dignify and glorify common labour and put brains and skill into the common occupation of life; shall prosper in proportion as we learn to draw the line between the superficial and the substantial, the ornamental gewgaws of life and the useful. No race can prosper till it learns that there is as much dignity in tilling a field as in writing a poem. It is at the bottom of life we must begin, and not at the top. Nor should we permit our grievances to overshadow our opportunities.

To those of the white race who look to the incoming of those of foreign birth and strange tongue and habits for the prosperity of the South, were I permitted I would repeat what I say to my own race, "Cast down your bucket where you are." Cast it down among the eight millions of Negroes whose habits you know, whose fidelity and love you have tested in days when to have proved treacherous meant the ruin of your firesides. Cast down your bucket among these people who have, without strikes and labour wars, tilled your fields, cleared your forests, builded your railroads and cities, and brought forth treasures from the bowels of the earth, and helped make possible this magnificent representation of the progress of the South. Casting down your bucket among my people, helping and encouraging them as you are doing on these grounds, and to education of head, hand, and heart, you will find that they will buy your surplus land, make blossom the waste places in your fields, and run your factories. While doing this, you can be sure in the future, as in the past, that you and your families will be surrounded by the most patient, faithful, law-abiding, and unresentful people that the world has seen. As we have proved our loyalty to you in the past, in nursing your children, watching by the sick-bed of your mothers and fathers, and often following them with tear-dimmed eyes to their graves, so in the future, in our humble way, we shall stand by you with a devotion that no foreigner can approach, ready to lay down our lives, if need be, in defence of yours, interlacing our industrial, commercial, civil, and religious life with yours in a way that shall make the interests of both races one. In all things that are purely social we can be as separate as the fingers, yet one as the hand in all things essential to mutual progress.

There is no defence or security for any of us except in the highest intelligence and development of all. If anywhere there are efforts tending to curtail the fullest growth of the Negro, let these efforts be turned into stimulating, encouraging, and making him the most useful and intelligent citizen. Effort or means so invested will pay a thousand per cent interest. These efforts will be twice blessed— "blessing him that gives and him that takes."

The wisest among my race understand that the agitation of questions of social equality is the extremest folly, and that progress in the enjoyment of all the privileges that will come to us must be the result of severe and constant struggle rather than of artificial forcing. No race that has anything to contribute to the markets of the world is long in any degree ostracized. It is important and right that all privileges of the law be ours, but it is vastly more important that we be prepared for the exercises of these privileges. The opportunity to earn a dollar in a factory just now is worth infinitely more than the opportunity to spend a dollar in an opera-house.

[Booker T. Washington, *Up from Slavery* (New York: Doubleday, Page & Co., 1902), pp. 218–24]

Document 2. W. E. B. Du Bois Disagrees with Washington

Educated at Fisk and Harvard Universities, W. E. B. Du Bois became the leader of blacks who disagreed with Washington's prescriptions. The passage below reflects Du Bois's disagreements with Washington.

Mr. Washington represents in Negro thought the old attitude of adjustment and submission; but adjustment at such a peculiar time as to make his programme unique. This is an age of unusual economic development, and Mr. Washington's programme naturally takes an economic cast, becoming a gospel of Work and Money to such an extent as apparently almost completely to overshadow the higher aims of life. Moreover, this is an age when the more advanced races are coming in closer contact with the less developed races, and the race-feeling is therefore intensified; and Mr. Washington's programme practically accepts the alleged inferiority of the Negro races. Again, in our own land, the reaction from the sentiment of war time has given impetus to race-prejudice against Negroes, and Mr. Washington withdraws many of the high demands of Negroes as men and American citizens. In other periods of intensified prejudice all the Negro's tendency to self-assertion has been called forth; at this period a policy of submission is advocated. In the history of nearly all other races and peoples the doctrine preached at such crises has been that manly self-respect is worth more than lands and houses, and that a people who voluntarily surrender such respect, or cease striving for it, are not worth civilizing.

In answer to this, it has been claimed that the Negro can survive only through submission. Mr. Washington distinctly asks that black people give up, at least for the present, three things—

First, political power,

Second, insistence on civil rights,

Third, higher education of Negro youth,—and concentrate all their energies on industrial education, the accumulation of wealth, and the conciliation of the South. This policy has been courageously and insistently advocated for over fifteen years, and has been trium-

phant for perhaps ten years. As a result of this tender of the palm-
branch, what has been the return? In these years there have occurred:

1. The disfranchisement of the Negro.

2. The legal creation of a distinct status of civil inferiority for the
Negro.

3. The steady withdrawal of aid from institutions for the higher
training of the Negro.

These movements are not, to be sure, direct results of Mr. Washington's teachings; but this propaganda has, without a shadow of
doubt, helped their speedier accomplishment. The question then
comes: Is it possible, and probable, that nine millions of men can
make effective progress in economic lines if they are deprived of
political rights, made a servile caste, and allowed only the most
meagre chance for developing their exceptional men? If history and
reason give any distinct answer to these questions, it is an emphatic
No. And Mr. Washington thus faces the triple paradox of his career:

1. He is striving nobly to make Negro artisans, businessmen and
property-owners; but it is utterly impossible, under modern competitive methods, for workingmen and property-owners to defend
their rights and exist without the right of suffrage.

2. He insists on thrift and self-respect, but at the same time counsels a silent submission to civic inferiority such as is bound to sap the
manhood of any race in the long run.

3. He advocates common-school and industrial training, and de-
preciates institutions of higher learning; but neither the Negro com-
mon-schools, nor Tuskegee itself, could remain open a day were it
not for teachers trained in Negro colleges, or trained by their gradu-
ates.

This triple paradox in Mr. Washington's position is the object of
criticism by two classes of colored Americans. One class is spiritually
descended from Toussaint the Savior, through Gabriel, Vesey, and
Turner, and they represent the attitude of revolt and revenge; they
hate the white South blindly and distrust the white race generally,
and so far as they agree on definite action, think that the Negro's
only hope lies in emigration beyond the borders of the United
States. And yet, by the irony of fate, nothing has more effectually
made this programme seem hopeless than the recent course of the
United States toward weaker and darker peoples in the West Indies,
Hawaii, and the Philippines,—for where in the world may we go
and be safe from lying and brute force?

The other class of Negroes who cannot agree with Mr. Washington has hitherto said little aloud. They deprecate the sight of scattered counsels, or internal disagreement; and especially they dislike
making their just criticism of a useful and earnest man an excuse for
a general discharge of venom from small-minded opponents. . . .
Such men feel in conscience bound to ask of this nation three things:

1. The right to vote.

2. Civic equality.

3. The education of youth according to ability.

They acknowledge Mr. Washington's invaluable service in coun-
selling patience and courtesy in such demands; they do not ask that
ignorant black men vote when ignorant whites are debarred, or that

any reasonable restrictions in the suffrage should not be applied; they know that the low social level of the mass of the race is responsible for much discrimination against it, but they also know, and the nation knows, that relentless color-prejudice is more often a cause than a result of the Negro's degradation; they seek the abatement of this relic of barbarism, and not its systematic encouragement and pampering by all agencies of social power from the Associated Press to the Church of Christ. They advocate, with Mr. Washington, a broad system of Negro common schools supplemented by thorough industrial training; but they are surprised that a man of Mr. Washington's insight cannot see that no such educational system ever has rested or can rest on any other basis than that of the well-equipped college and university, and they insist that there is a demand for a few such institutions throughout the South to train the best of the Negro youth as teachers, professional men, and leaders.

This group of men honor Mr. Washington for his attitude of conciliation toward the white South; they accept the "Atlanta Compromise" in its broadest interpretation; they recognize, with him, many signs of promise, many men of high purpose and fair judgment, in this section; they know that no easy task has been laid upon a region already tottering under heavy burdens. But, nevertheless, they insist that the way to truth and right lies in straightforward honesty, not in indiscriminate flattery; in praising those of the South who do well and criticising uncompromisingly those who do ill; in taking advantage of the opportunities at hand and urging their fellows to do the same, but at the same time in remembering that only a firm adherence to their higher ideals and aspirations will ever keep those ideals within the realm of possibility. They do not expect that the free right to vote, to enjoy civic rights, and to be educated, will come in a moment; they do not expect to see the bias and prejudices of years disappear at the blast of a trumpet; but they are absolutely certain that the way for a people to gain their reasonable rights is not by voluntarily throwing them away and insisting that they do not want them; that the way for a people to gain respect is not by continually belittling and ridiculing themselves; that, on the contrary, Negroes must insist continually, in season and out of season, that voting is necessary to modern manhood, that color discrimination is barbarism, and that black boys need education as well as white boys.

[W. E. B. Du Bois, "Of Mr. Booker T. Washington and Others," in *Souls of Black Folk* (Chicago: A. C. McClurg, 1903), pp. 50–55]

Questions for Reflection

What evidence do you see in Washington's speech that he was trying not to offend his predominantly white audience? Do you see evidence that Washington feared that blacks might be replaced by another group? What groups? How justified was his fear?

Does Du Bois seem to acknowledge the tightrope which Washington had to walk in developing his compromise position?

Are Du Bois's criticisms of Washington's position valid? Which of these men had a better concept of what blacks needed to do? Why?

ANSWERS TO MULTIPLE-CHOICE
AND TRUE-FALSE QUESTIONS

Multiple-Choice Questions

1-D, 2-A, 3-D, 4-B, 5-A, 6-D, 7-D, 8-B

True-False Questions

1-T, 2-T, 3-T, 4-F, 5-F, 6-T, 7-T.

20

THE RISE OF BIG BUSINESS

CHAPTER OBJECTIVES

After you complete the reading and study of this chapter, you should be able to:

1. Describe the economic impact of the Civil War.
2. Explain the important factors in the growth of the economy in the late nineteenth century.
3. Describe the role of the major entrepreneurs like Rockefeller, Carnegie, and Morgan.
4. Account for the limited growth of unions in this period, and the success of the Knights of Labor and the American Federation of Labor.
5. Describe the major labor confrontations in the period.
6. Account for the limited appeal of socialism for American labor.

CHAPTER OUTLINE

I. The post–Civil War economy
   A. Impact of the Civil War on the economy
      1. Early view of the impact
      2. Setbacks to the economy caused by the war
      3. Indirect effects of the Civil War
      4. Economic changes in the 1869–1899 period
   B. Railroad building
      1. Early federal aid to the railroads
      2. The transcontinental plan for the Central Pacific and the Union Pacific
      3. Other transcontinentals
      4. Financing the railroads
         a. Credit Mobilier fraud
         b. Government returns from the financial assistance given
      5. Jay Gould's work
      6. Cornelius Vanderbilt
      7. Railroads controlled by seven major groups
   C. New products and inventions
      1. Refrigerated railway car
      2. Flour milling
      3. Paper making
      4. Other improvements and inventions
      5. Development of the telephone
      6. Edison's work with electricity
   D. Entrepreneurs of the era
      1. Rockefeller and the oil industry
         a. Background
         b. Concentration on refining and transportation
         c. Development of the trust
         d. Evolution of the holding company
      2. Andrew Carnegie and the Gospel of Wealth

a. Background
b. Concentration on steel
c. Philosophy for big business
d. Other proponents of the Gospel of Wealth
3. J. P. Morgan and investment banking
a. Background
b. Concentration on railroad financing
c. Control of organizations
d. Consolidation of the steel industry
E. Impact of growth on the distribution of wealth

II. Developments in labor
A. Real wages and the work week
B. Living conditions
C. Control by impersonal forces
D. Violence in union activity
1. The Molly Maguires
2. The railroad strike of 1877
E. Efforts at union building
1. National Labor Union
2. Knights of Labor
a. Early development
b. Emphasis on the union

c. Role of Terrence Powderly
d. Victories of the Knights
e. Haymarket Affair
f. Lasting influence of the Knights of Labor
3. Development of the American Federation of Labor
a. Development of craft unions
b. Role of Samuel Gompers
c. Focus on the eight-hour day
d. Growth of the union
F. Violence in the 1890s
1. Homestead Strike, 1892
2. Pullman Strike, 1894
a. Causes
b. Role of the government
c. Impact on Eugene V. Debs
G. Socialism and American labor
1. Daniel Deleon and Eugene Debs
2. Social Democratic party
a. Early work
b. Height of influence
3. Rise of the IWW
a. Sources of strength
b. Revolutionary goals
c. Causes for decline
H. Generalization about American labor

KEY ITEMS OF CHRONOLOGY

National Labor Union formed	1866
Completion of the first transcontinental railroad	1869
Telephone patented	1876
Incandescent lightbulb invented	1879
Terrence Powderly became president of the Knights of Labor	1879
First electric current supplied to 85 customers in New York City	1882
Creation of the Standard Oil Trust	1882
Haymarket Affair	1886
Founding of the American Federation of Labor	1886
Pullman Strike	1894

TERMS TO MASTER

Listed below are some important terms or people with which you should be familiar after you complete the study of this chapter. Explain the significance of each name or term.

1. National Banking Act
2. transcontinental railroads
3. Crédit Mobilier
4. Cornelius Vanderbilt
5. Alexander Graham Bell
6. Thomas Alva Edison
7. George Westinghouse
8. John D. Rockefeller
9. Andrew Carnegie
10. Horatio Alger
11. J. Pierpont Morgan
12. United States Steel Company
13. *Gesellschaft*
14. Molly Maguires
15. National Labor Union
16. Knights of Labor
17. American Federation of Labor
18. Haymarket Affair
19. Samuel Gompers
20. Pullman Strike
21. Eugene V. Debs

VOCABULARY BUILDING

Listed below are some words or phrases used in this chapter. Look up each word in your dictionary unless the meaning is given here.

1. massif
2. probity
3. lexicon
4. watered stock
5. syndicalism

EXERCISES FOR UNDERSTANDING

When you have completed the reading of the chapter, answer each of the following questions. If you have difficulty, go back and reread the section of the chapter related to the question.

Multiple-Choice Questions

Select the letter of the response which best completes the statement.

1. The growth of output of American industry was
   A. significantly aided by the Civil War
   B. set back by the Civil War
   C. unaffected by the Civil War
   D. quadrupled by the Civil War

2. One way in which the Civil War did *not* help economic growth was
   A. creation of a national banking system
   B. encouragement of transcontinental railroads
   C. concentrating wealth in the hands of property owners
   D. reducing the demand for consumer goods

3. The profiteering of railroad companies included
   A. bribes to congressmen
   B. construction companies which overcharged for building railroads and made a profit
   C. shoddy workmanship in building the railroad lines
   D. all of the above

4. George Westinghouse is associated with
   A. the typewriter
   B. the electric range
   C. alternating current
   D. motion pictures

5. Rockefeller's guiding aim in the oil industry was to
   A. make more money than anyone else
   B. be able to give away more money than anyone else
   C. bring order out of the chaotic competition in the oil industry
   D. do all of the above

6. Andrew Carnegie
   A. made his fortune on toll bridges
   B. refused to give money directly to individuals; he preferred to found libraries
   C. believed in willing his wealth to be used in good causes only after his death
   D. thought it was wise to leave one's wealth to one's children

7. The Pullman Strike involved the
   A. loss of influence for the union because of association with anarchists
   B. use of Pinkerton detectives to break up the strike
   C. use of federal troops to ensure delivery of the mail
   D. bankruptcy of the Pullman Company
8. American workers tended to reject unions because
   A. they believed they would only be workers for a short time until they could own their own farms or move up otherwise
   B. they were so strongly committed to a system of equality and uniform wages for all
   C. they did not like the association with immigrants in unions
   D. they thought all unions were corrupt

True-False Questions

Indicate whether each statement is true or false.

1. According to Robert Gallman the Civil War caused a setback in the growth of commodity output in the United States.
2. J. P. Morgan wanted to eliminate the wasteful competition of the free-enterprise system.
3. In the late nineteenth century after the Civil War, *real* wages increased.
4. The AFL was primarily an industrial union.
5. Labor Day began as a celebration of Karl Marx's birthday.
6. The IWW had its roots in mining and lumbering camps.
7. The cigarmakers were the least influential of the craft unions.
8. By 1920 labor unions represented 50 percent of the nonagricultural workers.

Essay Questions

1. List and explain the factors that promoted the growth of industry in the United States in the late nineteenth century.
2. What characteristics do you find common among Rockefeller, Carnegie, and Morgan?
3. Describe and explain Carnegie's notion of the Gospel of Wealth.
4. Compare the five major labor incidents mentioned in the textbook: Molly Maguires, Railroad Strike of 1877, Haymarket Affair, Homestead Steel Strike, and Pullman Strike.
5. Explain why labor unions have always had a limited popularity in the United States as compared to other industrialized nations.

DOCUMENTS

Document 1. Andrew Carnegie Provides Rules for Disposing of Wealth

As the textbook indicates, Andrew Carnegie developed the concept of the Gospel of Wealth in an essay originally entitled "Wealth." Excerpted below are sections dealing with the best method for a person to use in disposing of his fortune.

It will be understood that *fortunes* are here spoken of, not moderate sums saved by many years of effort, the returns from which are required for the comfortable maintenance and education of families. This is not *wealth*, but only *competence*, which it should be the aim of all to acquire.

There are but three modes in which surplus wealth can be disposed of. It can be left to the families of the decedents; or it can be bequeathed for public purposes; or, finally, it can be administered

during their lives by its possessors. Under the first and second modes
most of the wealth of the world that has reached the few has hitherto been applied. Let us in turn consider each of these modes. The
first is the most injudicious. In monarchical countries, the estates
and the greatest portion of the wealth are left to the first son, that
the vanity of the parent may be gratified by the thought that his
name and title are to descend to succeeding generations unim-
paired. The condition of this class in Europe to-day teaches the
futility of such hopes or ambitions. The successors have become
impoverished through their follies or from the fall in the value of
land. . . . Under republican institutions the division of property
among the children is much fairer, but the question which forces
itself upon thoughtful men in all lands is: Why should men leave
great fortunes to their children? If this is done from affection, is it
not misguided affection? Observation teaches that, generally speaking, it is not well for the children that they should be so burdened.
Neither is it well for the State. Beyond providing for the wife and
daughters moderate sources of income, and very moderate allow-
ances indeed, if any, for the sons, men may well hesitate, for it is no
longer questionable that great sums bequeathed oftener work more
for the injury than for the good of the recipients. Wise men will soon
conclude that, for the best interests of the members of their families
and of the State, such bequests are an improper use of their means.

It is not suggested that men who have failed to educate their sons
to earn a livelihood cast them adrift in poverty. If any man has seen
fit to rear his sons with a view to their living idle lives, or, what is
highly commendable, has instilled in them the sentiment that they
are in a position to labor for public ends without reference to
pecuniary considerations, then, of course, the duty of the parent is
to see that such are provided for *in moderation.* There are instances
of millionaires' sons unspoiled by wealth, who, being rich, still perform great services in the community. Such are the very salt of the
earth, as valuable as, unfortunately, they are rare; still it is not the
exception, but the rule, that men must regard, and, looking at the
usual result of enormous sums conferred upon legatees, the
thoughtful man must shortly say, "I would as soon leave to my son
a curse as the almighty dollar," and admit to himself that it is not
the welfare of the children, but family pride, which inspires these
enormous legacies.

As to the second mode, that of leaving wealth at death for public
uses, it may be said that this is only a means for the disposal of
wealth, provided a man is content to wait until he is dead before he
becomes of much good in the world. Knowledge of the results of
legacies bequeathed is not calculated to inspire the brightest hopes
of much posthumous good being accomplished. The cases are not
few in which the real object sought by the testator is not attained,
nor are they few in which his real wishes are thwarted. In many
cases the bequests are so used as to become only monuments of his
folly. It is well to remember that it requires the exercise of no less
ability than that which acquired the wealth to use it so as to be really
beneficial to the community. Besides this, it may fairly be said that
no man is to be extolled for doing what he cannot help doing, nor
is he to be thanked by the community to which he only leaves

wealth at death. Men who leave vast sums in this way may fairly be thought men who would not have left it at all, had they been able to take it with them. The memories of such cannot be held in grateful remembrance, for there is no grace in their gifts. It is not to be wondered at that such bequests seem so generally to lack the blessing.

The growing disposition to tax more and more heavily large estates left at death is a cheering indication of the growth of a salutary change in public opinion. The State of Pennsylvania now takes—subject to some exceptions—one-tenth of the property left by its citizens. . . . Of all forms of taxation, this seems the wisest. Men who continue hoarding great sums all their lives, the proper use of which for public ends would work good to the community, should be made to feel that the community, in the form of the State, cannot thus be deprived of its proper share. By taxing estates heavily at death the State marks its condemnation of the selfish millionaire's unworthy life.

It is desirable that nations should go much further in this direction. Indeed, it is difficult to set bounds to the share of a rich man's estate which should go at his death to the public through the agency of the State, and by all means such taxes should be graduated, beginning at nothing upon moderate sums to dependents, and increasing rapidly as the amounts swell, until of the millionaire's hoard, as of Shylock's, at least

> The other half
> Comes to the privy coffer of the state.

This policy would work powerfully to induce the rich man to attend to the administration of wealth during his life, which is the end that society should always have in view, as being that by far the most fruitful for the people. Nor need it be feared that this policy would sap the root of enterprise and render men less anxious to accumulate, for to the class whose ambition it is to leave great fortunes and be talked about after their death, it will attract even more attention, and, indeed, be a somewhat nobler ambition to have enormous sums paid over to the state from their fortunes.

There remains, then, only one mode of using great fortunes; but in this we have the true antidote for the temporary unequal distribution of wealth, the reconciliation of the rich and the poor—a reign of harmony—another ideal, differing, indeed, from that of the Communist in requiring only the further evolution of existing conditions, not the total overthrow of our civilization. It is founded upon the present most intense individualism, and the race is prepared to put it in practice by degrees whenever it pleases. . . .

This, then, is held to be the duty of the man of Wealth: First, to set an example of modest, unostentatious living, shunning display or extravagance; to provide moderately for the legitimate wants of those dependent upon him; and after doing so to consider all surplus revenues which come to him simply as trust funds, which he is called upon to administer, and strictly bound as a matter of duty to administer in the manner which, in his judgment, is best calculated to produce the most beneficial results for the community—the man of wealth thus becoming the mere agent and trustee for his poorer brethen, bringing to their service his superior wisdom, experience, and ability to administer, doing for them better than they would or could do for themselves.

. . . It were better for mankind that the millions of the rich were thrown into the sea than so spent as to encourage the slothful, the drunken, the unworthy. Of every thousand dollars spent in so called charity to-day, it is probable that $950 is unwisely spent, so spent, indeed, as to produce the very evils which it proposes to mitigate or cure. A well-known writer of philosophic books admitted the other day that he had given a quarter of a dollar to a man who approached him as he was coming to visit the house of his friend. He knew nothing of the habits of this beggar, knew not the use that would be made of this money, although he had every reason to suspect that it would be spent improperly. This man professed to be a disciple of Herbert Spencer; yet the quarter-dollar given that night will probably work more injury than all the money which its thoughtless donor will ever be able to give in true charity will do good. He only gratified his own feelings, saved himself from annoyance—and this was probably one of the most selfish and very worst actions of his life, for in all respects he is most worthy.

In bestowing charity, the main consideration should be to help those who will help themselves; to provide part of the means by which those who desire to improve may do so; to give those who desire to rise the aids by which they may rise; to assist, but rarely or never to do all. Neither the individual nor the race is improved by alms-giving. Those worthy of assistance, except in rare cases, seldom require assistance. The really valuable men of the race never do, except in cases of accident or sudden change. Every one has, of course, cases of individuals brought to his own knowledge where temporary assistance can do genuine good, and these he will not overlook. But the amount which can be wisely given by the individual for individuals is necessarily limited by his lack of knowledge of the circumstances connected with each. He is the only true reformer who is as careful and as anxious not to aid the unworthy as he is to aid the worthy, and, perhaps, even more so, for in alms-giving more injury is probably done by rewarding vice than by relieving virtue.

[Andrew Carnegie, "Wealth," *North American Review* 148, no. 391 (June 1889): 657–63]

Document 2. Russell Conwell Encourages Christians to Obtain Wealth

In the sermon "Acres of Diamonds" which Russell Conwell delivered more than 6,000 times, he advised Christians to use their talent and energy to obtain wealth.

. . . I say you ought to be rich; you have no right to be poor. . . . You ought to be rich. But persons with certain religious prejudice will ask, "How can you spend your time advising the rising generation to give their time to getting money—dollars and cents—the commercial spirit?"

Yet I must say that you ought to spend time getting rich. You and I know there are some things more valuable than money; of course, we do. Ah, yes! By a heart made unspeakably sad by a grave on which the autumn leaves now fall, I know there are some things higher and grander and sublimer than money. Well does the man know, who has suffered, that there are some things sweeter and holier and more sacred than gold. Nevertheless, the man of common sense also knows that there is not one of those things that is not greatly enhanced by the use of money. Money is power. . . . Money is power; money has powers; and for a man to say, "I do not want money," is to say, "I do not wish to do any good to my fellowmen." It is absurd thus to talk. It is absurd to disconnect them. This is a wonderfully great life, and you ought to spend your time getting money, because of the power there is in money. And yet this religious prejudice is so great that some people think it is a great honor to be one of God's poor. . . . We ought to get rich if we can by honorable and Christian methods, and these are the only methods that sweep us quickly toward the goal of riches.

I remember, not many years ago a young theological student who came into my office and said to me that he thought it was his duty to come in and "labor with me." I asked what had happened, and he said: "I feel it is my duty to come in and speak to you, sir, and say that the Holy Scriptures declare that money is the root of all evil." I asked him where he found that saying, and he said he found it in the Bible. . . . So he took the Bible and read it: "The *love* of money is the root of all evil." . . . Oh, that is it. It is the worship of the means instead of the end, though you cannot reach the end without the means. When a man makes an idol of the money instead of the purposes for which it may be used, when he squeezes the dollar until the eagle squeals, then it is made the root of all evil. Think, if you only had the money, what you could do for your wife, your child, and for your home and your city.

[Agnes Rush Burr, *Russell H. Conwell, Founder of the Institutional Church in America: The Work and the Man* (Philadelphia: The John C. Winston Co., 1905), pp. 324–26]

Questions for Reflection

Has Carnegie listed all the methods for the disposal of fortunes? Would most wealthy people today agree with his notions of how to treat members of the family? How do you react to his notion of using the inheritance tax? Does it appear to you that most very wealthy people today follow his dictates for modest living? Is Carnegie right about the harm of almsgiving? What appear to be the sources for Carnegie's ideas? Are his concepts valid today or were they appropriate only for the nineteenth century, if that?

How does Russell Conwell's sermon reflect attitudes similar to Carnegie's? Is Conwell providing an appropriate reflection of the ethic of modern Christianity? How would Conwell's ideas be received by the wealthy people of his era? Why? Based on a reading of this portion of Conwell's sermon, how would you define the "gospel of wealth"?

ANSWERS TO MULTIPLE-CHOICE
AND TRUE-FALSE QUESTIONS

Multiple-Choice Questions

1-B, 2-D, 3-D, 4-C, 5-C, 6-B, 7-C, 8-A

True-False Questions

1-T, 2-T, 3-T, 4-F, 5-F, 6-T, 7-F, 8-F

21

THE EMERGENCE OF MODERN AMERICA

CHAPTER OBJECTIVES

After you complete the reading and study of this chapter, you should be able to:

1. Discuss the important intellectual trends in the period 1877–1890.
2. Describe city growth in the late nineteenth century.
3. Describe the new immigration and the reaction which it engendered.
4. Describe major developments in higher education after the Civil War.
5. Explain the concepts of Social Darwinism and Reform Darwinism.
6. Describe the local color, realist, and naturalist movements in literature.
7. Explain the social gospel and describe its manifestations.

CHAPTER OUTLINE

I. Urbanization
  A. Urbanization reflected in westward migration
  B. Factors important to urban prowess
  C. Characteristics of the new urban scene
  D. Vertical and horizontal growth of cities
    1. Development of elevators
    2. Development of cast-iron and steel-frame construction
    3. Development of electric streetcars
  E. Development of city planning
    1. Landscape architects and city parks
    2. Impact of Chicago Columbian Exposition, 1893–1894
    3. Planning in major cities
    4. Improvement of tenements
  F. Development of boss control
  G. Lure of the city

II. The new immigration
  A. Nature of the new immigrants
  B. Reasons for emigration to America
  C. Statistical impact of the new wave
  D. The nativist response
    1. Reasons for objection to new immigrants
    2. Rise of American Protective Association
  E. Efforts at immigration restriction

III. Growth of education
  A. Indication of the spread of schooling
  B. Nature of secondary education
  C. Growth of vocational education
  D. Vocational education at the college level
  E. Developments in higher education
    1. Growth of colleges
    2. Growth of the elective system
    3. Expansion of opportunities for women
    4. Development of graduate schools

F. The rise of professionalism
   1. Nature of the movement
   2. Fields developed
   3. Growth of professional societies

IV. Theories of social change
   A. Darwinism
      1. Darwin's ideas and their implications
      2. Social Darwinism
         a. Herbert Spencer's contributions
         b. John Fiske's ideas
         c. Popular science monthly
         d. William Graham Sumner's contributions
      3. Lester Frank Ward and Reform Darwinism
   B. Developments in other fields of learning
      1. Developments in history
      2. Sociology emerges
      3. Changes in economics
      4. Pragmatism
         a. Ideas of William James
         b. John Dewey and instrumentalism

V. Realism in American literature
   A. The local colorists
      1. Bret Harte
      2. Hamlin Garland
      3. George Washington Cable
      4. Joel Chandler Harris
      5. Thomas Nelson Page
   B. Mark Twain
   C. William Dean Howells
   D. Henry James
   E. Literary naturalism
      1. Frank Norris
      2. Stephen Crane
      3. Jack London
      4. Theodore Dreiser

VI. Social critics
   A. Henry George and the single tax
   B. Henry Demarest Lloyd and cooperation
   C. Thorstein Veblen and conspicuous consumption
   D. Edward Bellamy and the utopian novel

VII. The religious response: social gospel
   A. Abandonment of inner-city churches
   B. Development of the institutional church
      1. YMCA and the Salvation Army
      2. Institutional churches
   C. Washington Gladden
   D. Walter Rauschenbusch
   E. Catholic responses to modernity
      1. *Syllabus of Errors*
      2. *Rerum Novarum*

VIII. Early efforts at urban reform
   A. The settlement house movement
      1. Nature of settlement houses
      2. Social control
   B. Women's rights
      1. Growth of the female labor force
      2. Women's suffrage
         a. Conflicts in the movement
         b. Gains in the states
      3. Other women's efforts
   C. Efforts to regulate business
      1. State regulatory commissions
      2. Development of substantive due process
      3. Supreme Court acceptance of the view
         a. In cases against regulatory units
         b. In cases against labor
      4. The status of laissez-faire at the end of the century

KEY ITEMS OF CHRONOLOGY

Publication of *Popular Science Monthly*	1872
Founding of the Johns Hopkins University	1876
Publication of *Dynamic Sociology*	1883
Publication of *Huckleberry Finn*	1883
Stone v. Farmers' Loan and Trust Co.	1886
First electric elevator	1889
Electric streetcar systems in cities	1890s

Publication of *Maggie: A Girl of the Streets*	1893
Chicago Columbian Exposition	1893–1894
Smith v. Ames	1898

TERMS TO MASTER

Listed below are some important terms or people with which you should be familiar after you complete the study of this chapter. Explain the significance of each name or term.

1. Louis Sullivan
2. Frederick Law Olmstead
3. Columbian Exposition
4. dumbbell tenements
5. the new immigration
6. American Protective Association
7. Morrill Act of 1862
8. The Johns Hopkins University
9. Social Darwinism
10. Herbert Spencer
11. William Graham Sumner
12. Lester Frank Ward
13. "scientific" history
14. pragmatism
15. John Dewey
16. Mark Twain
17. Henry James
18. naturalism
19. Henry George
20. Edward Bellamy
21. Social Gospel
22. settlement houses
23. Susan B. Anthony

VOCABULARY BUILDING

Listed below are some words or phrases used in this chapter. Look up each word in your dictionary unless the meaning is given here.

1. salubrious
2. infrastructure
3. xenophobia
4. nemesis

EXERCISES FOR UNDERSTANDING

When you have completed the reading of the chapter, answer each of the following questions. If you have difficulty, go back and reread the section of the chapter related to the question.

Multiple-Choice Questions

Select the letter of the response which best completes the statement.

1. Cities in the late nineteenth century
   A. grew faster in the South than in the North
   B. were proportionately a greater part of the population in the Far West than in any other region
   C. grew upward, but not outward
   D. grew larger; but no new ones developed

2. Frederick Law Olmstead was
   A. a city boss
   B. an architect of skyscrapers
   C. a landscape architect who designed parks
   D. a pragmatist philosopher

3. The dumbbell tenements
   A. allowed more people to own their own homes
   B. were more fireproof than earlier tenements
   C. allowed more ventilation than earlier tenements
   D. limited the number of persons who could occupy a room

4. The new immigration after 1880 came mainly from
   A. southern and eastern Europe
   B. Asia and northern Europe
   C. Germany and Ireland
   D. Italy and Scandinavia

5. The Morrill Act of 1862
   A. allowed land to be given for building liberal arts colleges in each state

B. provided federal funds for scholarships
C. promoted building agricultural and mechanical colleges
D. forbade attendance at colleges by blacks

6. Spencer's ideas supported
   A. reform of business organization
   B. slum-clearance projects
   C. belief in the ultimate perfection of human society
   D. the need for better planning to direct social development

7. Henry George believed all social ills could be solved by
   A. an income tax
   B. socialization of all private property
   C. a tax on unearned increment
   D. a tax on the number of windows in a house

8. The social gospel encouraged
   A. assistance to middle-class Christians
   B. a focus on personal sins
   C. the development of the Kingdom of God here on earth
   D. the laissez-faire business philosophy

True-False Questions

Indicate whether each statement is true or false.

1. The great immigration into the United States in the late nineteenth century was part of the movement from the country to the city.
2. Political bosses of the late nineteenth century performed many services provided later by social workers.
3. The new immigrants were less clannish than the earlier immigrants.

4. Higher education in the late nineteenth century allowed more flexibility in the curriculum than previously.
5. Darwin's ideas seem to contradict the literal interpretation of the book of Genesis in the Bible.
6. The idea of "scientific" history was based on the belief that events could be reproduced exactly as they had occurred.
7. Mark Twain is an excellent example of a naturalist writer.
8. Substantive due process used the Fourteenth Amendment to protect businesses from regulation.

Essay Questions

1. Describe the process of urbanization in the late nineteenth century.
2. Account for the development of the city planning movement and show some of its effects.
3. Explain the reasons for the new immigration after 1880.
4. Was higher education weakened or strengthened by the educational changes of the late nineteenth century?
5. Explain the concept of Social Darwinism and describe its impact.
6. What elements of Darwinism were apparent in the developments in history, sociology, economics, and philosophy?
7. What characterized the local color, realist, and naturalist schools of literature in America?
8. Define the Social Gospel and account for the rise of the movement.
9. What is meant by substantive due process, and why is it important?

DOCUMENT

Circumstances of Typical Illinois Working Families

In 1884 the Illinois Bureau of Labor Statistics conducted a survey of typical laboring families. The survey included over 2,000 families, of whom 167 were selected for detailed accounts. Excerpted here are the accounts of four families diverse in occupation, income, and circumstances.

In order to present a closer view of the manner of living, the surroundings, habits, tastes and daily diet of the Illinois workingman of to-day, under various circumstances and conditions, and to afford a more definite impression as to the details of his environment than can be obtained from the mere contemplation of columns of figures, we transcribe, for a limited number of representative families, their entire record, as procured by our agents, together with the notes of observation, made at the time of the visit. . . .

This minute catalogue of the details governing the life of each family portrays more vividly than any mere array of figures can the common current of daily life among the people. The extremes of condition and the average types are alike presented, and it may be seen, not only what manner of life ordinarily prevails with a given income, but also how some families, by thrift, temperance and prudence, save money and increase their store, upon earnings which other families find insufficient for their support. . . .

No. 2   Baker   Pole

Earnings—Of father $450

Condition—Family numbers 5—parents and three children, all girls, aged one month, eighteen months and four years. Rent a house containing three rooms, for which they pay a rental of $8 per month. Family are very ignorant, dirty and unkempt. The street is narrow and filthy: no pavement: mud knee-deep: no vaults or sewerage. Father works fifty weeks per year, and for a winter day's work he is employed twelve hours, and in summer fourteen. He receives $1.50 for each day's labor. His house is situated so far from his place of work that he cannot go home at noon. Carries no life insurance, and belongs to no unions.

Food—Breakfast—Coffee, bread and crackers.
       Dinner—Soup, meat and potatoes.
       Supper—What is left from dinner.

Cost of Living—

Rent	$96
Fuel	15
Meat and groceries	165
Clothing, boots and shoes and dry goods	70
Books, papers, etc.	3
Sickness	40
Sundries	65
Total	$454

No. 21   Cigarmaker   Bohemian

Earnings—Of father $450
          Of son   750
          Of son   600
                        $1,830

Condition—Family numbers 7—four boys and one girl. The boys pay for their board to their parents, clothe themselves, and otherwise aid in the support of the family. They occupy a house containing 6 rooms, for which they pay $12 per month rent. The father is a member of the trades union, and considers himself and family benefited thereby. House is in healthy location, fairly furnished, with 3 of the rooms carpeted. With the assistance of the boys they are enabled to save a little money each year.

Food—Breakfast—Meat, coffee, bread, butter and potatoes.
Dinner—Meat, vegetables, soup, etc.
Supper—Cold meat, tea, bread and butter.

Cost of Living—

Rent	$144
Fuel	80
Meat	100
Groceries	300
Clothing	200
Boots and shoes	60
Dry goods	$200
Books, papers, etc.	20
Trades unions	12
Sickness	75
Sundries	100
Total	$1,291

No. 35   Laborer   Italian

Earnings—Of father $270

Condition—Family numbers 5—parents and three children, all boys, aged one, three and five. Live in one room, for which they pay $4 per month rent. A very dirty and unhealthy place, everything perfectly filthy. There are about fifteen other families living in the same house. They buy the cheapest kind of meat from the neighboring slaughter houses and the children pick up fuel on the streets and rotten eatables from the comission houses. Children do not attend school. They are all ignorant in the full sense of the word. Father could not write his name.

Food—Breakfast—Coffee, and bread.
Dinner—Soups.
Supper—Coffee and bread.

Cost of Living—

Rent	$48
Fuel	5
Meat and groceries	100
Clothing, boots and shoes and dry goods	15
Sickness	5
Total	$173

No. 112   Coal Miner   American

Earnings—Of father $250

Condition—Family numbers 7—husband, wife, and five children, three girls and two boys, aged from three to nineteen years. Three of them go to the public school. Family live in 2 rooms tenement, in healthy locality, for which they pay $6 per month rent. The house is scantily furnished, without carpets, but is kept neat and clean. They are compelled to live very economically, and every cent they earn is used to the best advantage. Father had only thirty weeks work during the past year. He belongs to trades union. The figures for cost of living are actual and there is no doubt the family lived on the amount specified.

Food—Breakfast—Bread, coffee and salt meat.
       Dinner—Meat, bread, coffee and butter.
       Supper—Sausage, bread and coffee.

Cost of Living—

Rent	$72
Fuel	20
Meat	20
Groceries	60
Clothing	28
Boots and Shoes	15
Dry goods	$20
Trades unions	3
Sickness	10
Sundries	5
Total	$252

[Illinois Bureau of Labor Statistics, "Earnings, Expenses and Conditions of Workingmen and Their Families," *Third Biennial Report* (Springfield, Ill., 1884), reprinted in *The Transformation of American Society, 1870–1890,* edited by John A. Garraty (New York: Harper and Row, 1968), pp. 120–21, 124–25, 132]

Questions for Reflection

How do you account for the ability of some families to live on only $173 or $252 per year while other families needed $454 or $1,231? Which budget category varied the most among these families? Which categories were added when families were more affluent? Which families showed savings and which showed deficits? What factors appear to have influenced family income the most? Now that you have examined this information, if someone asked you how much it cost for a family to live in the late nineteenth century, how would you answer?

What conclusions can you draw about urban life in the 1880s?

ANSWERS TO MULTIPLE-CHOICE
AND TRUE-FALSE QUESTIONS

Multiple-Choice Questions

1-B, 2-C, 3-C, 4-A, 5-C, 6-C, 7-C, 8-C

True-False Questions

1-T, 2-T, 3-F, 4-T, 5-T, 6-T, 7-F, 8-T

22

GILDED AGE POLITICS AND AGRARIAN REVOLT

CHAPTER OBJECTIVES

After you complete the reading and study of this chapter, you should be able to:

1. Describe the major features of politics in the late nineteenth century.
2. Describe the political alignments and issues in the "third political system."
3. Explain the major issues in the presidential elections of 1888, 1892, and 1896.
4. Account for the rise of the farmer protest movement of the 1890s.
5. Explain the impact of populism on the American scene.

CHAPTER OUTLINE

I. Nature of Gilded Age politics
   A. Locus of real power
   B. Mediocre men in public office
   C. Nature of political parties
      1. Evaded stands on most issues
      2. Some distinction on tariff issue
      3. Patronage important to each party
      4. Coalitions of diverse interests in each party
      5. Reasons for evasiveness of parties
         a. Fear of repetition of split of 1860

      b. Even division between parties in popular vote (1868–1912)
      6. Few decisive new programs
      7. Availability of candidates outweighed ability
      8. Close alliance of business and politics characterized the age
   D. Nature of the "third political system"
      1. Not in mold of self-interest and economic motivation
      2. Higher voter participation
      3. Public belief in the reality of the issues
      4. Intense cultural conflicts
      5. Republic party characterized
      6. Democratic party characterized
      7. Resurgence of nativism
      8. Revival of prohibitionism

II. The Hayes administration
   A. His background and upright character
   B. Republic splits between Stalwarts and Half-Breeds
   C. Need for civil service reform
      1. Hayes's payment of political debts
      2. Supporters of reform
   D. Hayes's executive rules for merit appointments
   E. Problems with the New York customs house
   F. Hayes's limited version of government activitism

III. The election of 1880
    A. Republican nomination
        1. The Grant candidacy
        2. Garfield's nomination as a dark
           horse
    B. Democratic nomination of Winfield
       Scott Hancock
    C. Closest election results of the century

IV. The Garfield-Arthur administration
    A. Garfield's background
    B. His clash with Boss Platt over
       appointments
    C. His assassination
    D. Arthur's background
    E. His strong actions as president
        1. Prosecution of Star Route Frauds
        2. Veto of Rivers and Harbors Bill
        3. Veto of Chinese Exclusion Act
        4. Support of Pendleton Civil Service
           Act, 1883
        5. Support for tariff reduction
           a. Effects of treasury surplus
           b. Nature of the Mongrel Tariff of
              1883
    F. Scurrilous campaign of 1884
        1. Reasons Arthur was not a
           candidate
        2. Republican nomination of Blaine
           and Logan
           a. Blaine's background
           b. Effect of Mulligan letters
           c. Emergence of "Mugwumps"
        3. Democratic nomination of
           Cleveland
           a. Cleveland's political background
           b. His illegitimate child
           c. Concept of "Rum, Romanism,
              and Rebellion"
        4. Election results

V. Cleveland's presidency
    A. Cleveland's view of the role of
       government
    B. His actions on civil service
    C. His stand for conservation
    D. His stand against veterans' pensions
    E. His effort to return Confederate battle
       flags
    F. His effort for railroad legislation
    G. His stand for tariff reform
    H. Election of 1888
        1. Cleveland renominated

        2. Republican nomination of
           Benjamin Harrison
        3. Campaign focuses on the tariff
        4. Personal attacks
        5. Results

VI. Republican reform under Harrison
    A. Harrison's bland personality
    B. His appointments
    C. Republican control of Congress,
       1889–1891
    D. Passage of Sherman Antitrust Act,
       1890
    E. Sherman Silver Purchase Act, 1890
    F. Effect of McKinley Tariff, 1890
    G. Democratic congressional victories of
       1890
        1. Ostensible reaction to heavy
           spending of Republicans
        2. Impact on the election of
           prohibition and social issues

VII. Problems of farmers
    A. Worsening economic and social
       conditions
        1. Causes for declining agricultural
           prices
           a. Overproduction
           b. Worldwide competition
         2. The railroads as villains
        3. Effects of the tariff on farmers
        4. Problems of currency deflation
           a. Decrease of currency in
              circulation
           b. Impact of greenbacks
           c. Reasons for the focus on free
              silver
        5. Problems of geography and
           climate
        6. Isolation of farmers
    B. Development of Patrons of
       Husbandry
        1. Development of the Grange
        2. Effects of Granger political
           activity
    C. Rise of the Greenback party
    D. Emergence of Farmers' Alliances
    E. Alliances' entry into politics
    F. Formation of the Populist party
        1. Development of the party
        2. Platform stands
        3. Presidential nominees
        4. Victory of Cleveland in 1892

VIII. Depression of 1893
   A. Nature of the depression
   B. Reactions to the depression
   C. Results of the 1894 elections

IX. Focus on silver
   A. The causes and effects of the gold drain
   B. Agitation for free silver

    1. American Bimetallic League
    2. *Coin's Financial School*
   C. Effect on nominations of 1896
    1. Republican actions
    2. Democratic candidate
    3. Populist position
   D. Campaign of 1896 and its results
   E. The postelection shift to gold

KEY ITEMS OF CHRONOLOGY

Patrons of Husbandry founded	1867
Pendleton Civil Service Act	1883
Mongrel Tariff Act	1883
Interstate Commerce Act	1887
Sherman Antitrust Act	1890
Sherman Silver Purchase Act	1890
McKinley Tariff Act	1890
Populist party founded	1890
Hayes administration	1877–1881
Garfield administration	March–September 1881
Arthur administration	September 1881–1885
Cleveland administrations	1885–1889; 1893–1897
Benjamin Harrison administration	1889–1893
McKinley administrations	1897–1901

TERMS TO MASTER

Listed below are some important terms or people with which you should be familiar after you complete the study of this chapter. Explain significance of each name or term.

1. Stalwarts
2. Half-Breeds
3. Bland-Allison Act
4. Pendleton Civil Service Act (1883)
5. "Mongrel Tariff" of 1883
6. James G. Blaine
7. Mugwumps
8. Grand Army of the Republic (GAR)
9. *Wabash Railroad v. Illinois*
10. Sherman Antitrust Act
11. Sherman Silver Purchase Act
12. McKinley Tariff
13. "free and unlimited coinage of silver"
14. Patrons of Husbandry
15. Farmers' Alliances
16. Populist party
17. Jacob S. Coxey
18. William H. Harvey

VOCABULARY BUILDING

Listed below are some words or phrases used in this chapter. Look up each word in your dictionary unless the meaning is given here.

1. humbuggery
2. heterogeneous
3. besmirched

EXERCISES FOR UNDERSTANDING

When you have completed the reading of the chapter, answer each of the following questions. If you have difficulty, go back and reread the section of the chapter related to the question.

Multiple-Choice Questions

Select the letter of the response which best completes the statement.

1. The political parties from 1870 to 1896 generally
   A. disagreed about the issue of civil service reform
   B. pursued a policy of evasion on all issues
   C. most closely agreed with each other in the issue of the tariff
   D. disagreed most strongly over the regulation of business

2. As compared with the present, voter participation in the Gilded Age was
   A. much greater than now
   B. much less than now
   C. about the same as now
   D. a requirement

3. Which of the following is true of political control in the late nineteenth century?
   A. For only four years of this time did a Republican control both the presidency and the Congress
   B. The Democrats never controlled both the presidency and Congress
   C. From 1872 to 1896 only one president failed to win a decisive majority of the popular vote
   D. More Democrats than Republicans controlled the presidency

4. Prohibition tended to be favored more by the
   A. Republicans
   B. Democrats
   C. Populists
   D. European immigrant groups

5. The Star Route Frauds involved
   A. undercover payments for railroad construction contracts
   B. corruption in the awarding of pensions to Union veterans
   C. nonpayment of tariffs on certain trade routes to the Orient
   D. kickbacks on postal rates in the southwestern United States

6. Which of the following was *not* one of the actions of Cleveland as president?
   A. efforts to add pensions for Confederate veterans
   B. restoration to the public domain of exploited public lands in the West
   C. efforts to reduce the tariff
   D. creation of an agency to regulate railroads and other interstate commerce

7. Farmers believed that free coinage of silver would bring about
   A. lower prices for goods they needed to buy
   B. lower interest rates on loans
   C. higher prices for their farm products
   D. higher tariffs to protect their farm products from competition from abroad

8. Bryan lost the election of 1896 because of *all but which one* of the following?
   A. He failed to gain support of metropolitan areas of the East
   B. Ethnic voters were repelled by his flamboyant style
   C. Eastern farmers were not hurting like those of the South and West
   D. Support of industrial leaders caused workingmen to desert his cause

True-False Questions

Indicate whether each statement is true or false.

1. Party loyalty and voter turnout in the Gilded Age were primarily motivated by intense cultural conflicts among ethnic groups.
2. As president, Hayes opposed all efforts for civil service reform.
3. The Democratic party generally favored a lower tariff than the Republicans.
4. The Pendleton Civil Service Act provided for the filling of all future government positions on the basis of merit examinations.

5. The outcome of the election of 1892 was affected by efforts to legislate prohibition and oppose parochial schools.
6. The Southern Farmers' Alliance most often sought to support the Republican party.
7. Inflation came in the McKinley administration because of the president's efforts to increase the tariff.

Essay Questions

1. Compare the Democratic and Republican parties' stands on issues during the late nineteenth century. Indicate the groups to which each party attempted to appeal.
2. How did Arthur's presidency prove different from the expectations of many?
3. Explain the role played in Republican presidential politics by James G. Blaine. Why was Blaine never elected president?
4. What were the major issues which Cleveland supported as president? Why was he not more successful as president?
5. What were the major accomplishments of the Harrison administration? How did he manage to secure so much legislative action? What were the effects of this legislation?
6. Account for the farmer protest movement and trace its development from the Civil War to 1896.
7. How was the farmer protest movement in the South different from that in the rest of the nation? Why?

DOCUMENT

The Omaha Platform of the Populist Party

The platform adopted by the Populist Party in 1892 shows what the Populists thought was wrong with America and how they proposed to remedy these ills.

National People's Party
Platform

Assembled upon the 116th anniversary of the Declaration of Independence, the People's Party of America, in their first national convention, invoking upon their action the blessing of Almighty God, put forth in the name and on behalf of the people of this country, the following preamble and declaration of principles:

Preamble

The conditions which surround us best justify our co-operation; we meet in the midst of a nation brought to the verge of moral, political, and material ruin. Corruption dominates the ballot-box, the Legislatures, the Congress, and touches even the ermine of the bench. The people are demoralized; most of the States have been compelled to isolate the voters at the polling places to prevent universal intimidation and bribery. The newspapers are largely subsidized or muzzled, public opinion silenced, business prostrated, homes covered with mortgages, labor impoverished, and the land concentrating in the hands of capitalists. The urban workmen are denied the right to organize for self-protection, imported pauperized labor beats down their wages, a hireling standing army, unrecognized by our laws, is established to shoot them down, and they are rapidly degenerating into European conditions. The fruits of the toil of millions are boldly stolen to build up colossal fortunes for a few, unprecedented in the history of mankind; and the possessors of those, in turn, despite the Republic and endanger liberty. From the same prolific womb of governmental injustice we breed the two great classes—tramps and millionaires.

The national power to create money is appropriated to enrich bondholders; a vast public debt payable in legal tender currency has been funded into gold-bearing bonds, thereby adding millions to the burdens of the people.

Silver, which has been accepted as coin since the dawn of history, has been demonetized to add to the purchasing power of gold by decreasing the value of all forms of property as well as human labor, and the supply of currency is purposely abridged to fatten usurers, bankrupt enterprise, and enslave industry. A vast conspiracy against mankind has been organized on two continents, and it is rapidly taking possession of the world. If not met and overthrown at once it forebodes terrible social convulsions, the destruction of civilization, or the establishment of an absolute despotism.

We have witnessed for more than a quarter of a century the struggles of the two great political parties for power and plunder, while grievous wrongs have been inflicted upon the suffering people. We charge that the controlling influences dominating both these parties have permitted the existing dreadful conditions to develop without serious effort to prevent or restrain them. Neither do they now promise us any substantial reform. They have agreed together to ignore, in the coming campaign, every issue but one. They propose to drown the outcries of a plundered people with the uproar of a sham battle over the tariff, so that capitalists, corporations, national banks, rings, trusts, watered stock, the demonetization of silver and the oppressions of the usurers may all be lost sight of. They propose to sacrifice our homes, lives, and children on the altar of mammon; to destroy the multitude in order to secure corruption funds from the millionaires.

Assembled on the anniversary of the birthday of the nation, and filled with the spirit of the grand general and chief who established our independence, we seek to restore the government of the Republic to the hands of "the plain people," with which class it originated. We assert our purposes to be identical with the purposes of the National Constitution; to form a more perfect union and establish justice, insure domestic tranquility, provide for the common defence, promote the general welfare, and secure the blessings of liberty for ourselves and our posterity.

We declare that this Republic can only endure as a free government while built upon the love of the whole people for each other and for the nation; that it cannot be pinned together by bayonets; that the civil war is over, and that every passion and resentment which grew out of it must die with it, and that we must be in fact, as we are in name, one united brotherhood of free men.

Our country finds itself confronted by conditions for which there is no precedent in the history of the world; our annual agricultural productions amount to billions of dollars in value, which must, within a few weeks or months, be exchanged for billions of dollars' worth of commodities consumed in their production; the existing currency supply is wholly inadequate to make this exchange; the results are falling prices, the formation of combines and rings, the impoverishment of the producing class. We pledge ourselves that if given power we will labor to correct these evils by wise and reasonable legislation, in accordance with the terms of our platform.

We believe that the power of government—in other words, of the people—should be expanded (as in the case of the postal service) as rapidly and as far as the good sense of an intelligent people and the teachings of experience shall justify, to the end that oppression, injustice, and poverty shall eventually cease in the land.

While our sympathies as a party of reform are naturally upon the side of every proposition which will tend to make men intelligent, virtuous, and temperate, we nevertheless regard these questions, important as they are, as secondary to the great issues now pressing for solution, and upon which not only our individual prosperity but the very existence of free institutions depend; and we ask all men to first help us to determine whether we are to have a republic to administer before we differ as to the conditions upon which it is to be administered, believing that the forces of reform this day organized will never cease to move forward until every wrong is remedied and equal rights and equal privileges securely established for all the men and women of this country.

Platform

We declare, therefore—

First.—That the union of the labor forces of the United States this day consummated shall be permanent and perpetual; may its spirit enter into all hearts for the salvation of the Republic and the uplifting of mankind.

Second.—Wealth belongs to him who creates it, and every dollar taken from industry without an equivalent is robbery. "If any will not work, neither shall he eat." The interests of rural and civic labor are the same; their enemies are identical.

Third.—We believe that the time has come when the railroad corporations will either own the people or the people must own the railroads, and should the government enter upon the work of owning and managing all railroads, we should favor an amendment to the Constitution by which all persons engaged in the government service shall be placed under a civil-service regulation of the most rigid character, so as to prevent the increase of the power of the national administration by the use of such additional government employes.

Finance.—We demand a national currency safe, sound, and flexible, issued by the general government only, a full legal tender for all debts, public and private, and that without the use of banking corporations, a just, equitable, and efficient means of distribution direct to the people, at a tax not to exceed 2 per cent per annum, to be provided as set forth in the sub-treasury plan of the Farmers' Alliance, or a better system; also by payments in discharge of its obligations for public improvements.

1. We demand free and unlimited coinage of silver and gold at the present legal ratio of 16 to 1.

2. We demand that the amount of circulating medium be speedily increased to not less than $50 per capita.

3. We demand a graduated income tax.

4. We believe that the money of the country should be kept as much as possible in the hands of the people, and hence we demand that all State and national revenues shall be limited to the necessary expenses of the government, economically and honestly administered.

5. We demand that postal savings banks be established by the government for the safe deposit of the earnings of the people and to facilitate exchange.

Transportation.—Transportation being a means of exchange and a public necessity, the government should own and operate the railroads in the interest of the people. The telegraph, telephone, like the post-office system, being a necessity for the transmission of news, should be owned and operated by the government in the interest of the people.

Land.—The land, including all the natural sources of wealth, is the heritage of the people, and should not be monopolized for speculative purposes, and alien ownership of land should be prohibited. All land now held by railroads and other corporations in excess of their actual needs, and all lands now owned by aliens should be reclaimed by the government and held for actual settlers only.

Expression of Sentiments

Your Committee on Platform and Resolutions beg leave unanimously to report the following:

Whereas, Other questions have been presented for our consideration, we hereby submit the following, not as a part of the Platform of the People's Party, but as resolutions expressive of the sentiment of the Convention.

1. *Resolved,* That we demand a free ballot and a fair count in all elections, and pledge ourselves to secure it to every legal voter without Federal intervention, through the adoption by the States of the unperverted Australian or secret ballot system.

2. *Resolved,* That the revenue derived from a graduated income tax should be applied to the reduction of the burden of taxation now levied upon the domestic industries of this country.

3. *Resolved,* That we pledge our support to fair and liberal pensions to ex-Union soldiers and sailors.

4. *Resolved,* That we condemn the fallacy of protecting American labor under the present system, which opens our ports to the pauper and criminal classes of the world and crowds out our wage-earners; and we denounce the present ineffective laws against contract labor, and demand the further restriction of undesirable emigration.

5. *Resolved,* That we cordially sympathize with the efforts of organized workingmen to shorten the hours of labor, and demand a rigid enforcement of the existing eight-hour law on Government work, and ask that a penalty clause be added to the said law.

6. *Resolved,* That we regard the maintenance of a large standing army of mercenaries, known as the Pinkerton system, as a menace to our liberties, and we demand its abolition; and we condemn the recent invasion of the Territory of Wyoming by the hired assassins of plutocracy, assisted by Federal officers.

7. *Resolved,* That we commend to the favorable consideration of the people and the reform press the legislative system known as the initiative and referendum.

8. *Resolved,* That we favor a constitutional provision limiting the office of President and Vice-President to one term, and providing for the election of Senators of the United States by a direct vote of the people.

9. *Resolved,* That we oppose any subsidy or national aid to any private corporation for any purpose.

10. *Resolved,* That this convention sympathizes with the Knights of Labor and their righteous contest with the tyrannical combine of clothing manufacturers of Rochester, and declare it to be the duty of all who hate tyranny and oppression to refuse to purchase the goods made by the said manufacturers, or to patronize any merchants who sell such goods.

[*The World Almanac,* 1893 (New York: Publisher, 1893), pp. 83–85, reprinted in *A Populist Reader,* edited by George B. Tindall (New York: Harper and Row, 1966), pp. 90–96]

Questions for Reflection

What ideas expressed in the preamble do you recognize from your study of this period? (For example, the "hireling standing army" refers to the Pinkerton detectives often used in cases of industrial violence.

Which planks of the platform and expressions of sentiments were later enacted in one form or another?

ANSWERS TO MULTIPLE-CHOICE AND TRUE-FALSE QUESTIONS

Multiple-Choice Questions

1-B, 2-A, 3-A, 4-A, 5-D, 6-A, 7-C, 8-D

True-False Questions

1-T, 2-F, 3-T, 4-F, 5-T, 6-F, 7-F

23

THE COURSE OF EMPIRE

CHAPTER OBJECTIVES

After you complete the reading and study of this chapter, you should be able to:

1. Explain why the United States entered upon a policy of imperialism.
2. Account for the outbreak of the Spanish-American War.
3. Explain the course of United States relations with Latin America during the late nineteenth century and its impact on later relations with Latin America.
4. Contrast the arguments for and against imperialism in 1899.
5. Explain the development of America's policy to deal with its imperial possessions.
6. Account for the acquisition of the Panama Canal.
7. Assess the foreign policies of Theodore Roosevelt and William Howard Taft.

CHAPTER OUTLINE

I. Stirrings of imperialism
  A. Isolationism prior to the Civil War
  B. Seward's diplomacy
    1. Napoleon III's Mexican adventure (1867)
    2. Purchase of Alaska (1867)
    3. Annexation of Midway Islands (1867)

  C. Fish's settlements of claims with Britain (1871)
  D. Expansionist visions in the Pacific
    1. Early whaling and missionary interests
    2. Acquisition of Samoa
    3. Relations with Hawaii
      a. Early American settlements
      b. Reciprocal trade agreement of 1875
      c. Constitutional government
      d. Dole revolution and desire for annexation (1893)
      e. Hawaii proclaimed a republic (1894)

II. Motivation for imperialism
  A. Economic motivations
  B. Mahan's concept of sea power
  C. Social Darwinian justifications
    1. Concept of Social Darwinism
    2. Racial corollaries
  D. Religious justification

III. Formation of ties with Latin America
  A. Role of James G. Blaine
  B. Efforts to develop ties with Latin American states

IV. Problems in the Western Hemisphere
  A. Dispute over sealing in the Bering Sea
  B. Conflicts with Chile
  C. Venezuelan boundary dispute
    1. Basis for Venezuela's conflict with Britain

2. United States' efforts to obtain arbitration

3. Final settlement by arbitration

V. Development of the Spanish-American War
  A. Effects of American investments and tariffs
  B. Guerrilla warfare by revolutionaries
  C. Wyler's reconcentration policy
  D. Role of the press in the war
    1. Contest between Hearst's *Journal* and Pulitzer's *World*
    2. Examples of yellow journalism
  E. Cleveland's efforts for compromise
  F. Spanish response to McKinley's stance
  G. Arousal of public opinion
    1. de Lome letter (Feb. 9, 1898)
    2. Sinking of the *Maine* (Feb. 15, 1898)
  H. The final moves to war
  I. Motives for war

VI. Fighting the "splendid little war"
  A. Role of war correspondents
  B. Naval victory at Manila Bay
  C. Cuban blockade
    1. Problems of the army
    2. The Rough Riders
    3. Seige of Santiago
  D. Puerto Rican campaign
  E. Terms of the armistice

VII. Developing and debating imperialism
  A. Negotiations for the Treaty of Paris (Dec. 10)
    1. Cuban debt question
    2. Annexation of the Philippines
  B. Motives for annexation
  C. Terms of the treaty
  D. Other territorial acquisitions
  E. Debate over the treaty
    1. Anti-imperialist arguments
    2. Bryan's support
    3. Ratification (February 1899)
  F. Filipino insurrection
  G. Emergence of the Anti-Imperialist League (October 1899)

VIII. Election of 1900
  A. Democrats focus on imperialism
  B. Republican nominees
  C. Outcome of the election
  D. McKinley's assassination
  E. TR's background and character

IX. Organizing the new acquisitions
  A. The Philippines under Taft
  B. Civil government for Puerto Rico
  C. The Insular Cases
    1. The questions at issue
    2. Lack of incorporation for overseas possessions
  D. Problems in Cuba
    1. Leonard Wood as military governor
    2. Efforts to control yellow fever
    3. Cuban constitution
    4. Platt Amendment
    5. Insurrection of 1906

X. Imperial rivalries in the Far East
  A. Japan's modernization
  B. The scramble for spheres of influence in China
  C. The Open-Door Policy
    1. British initiatives
    2. Unilateral action
    3. Policies of the Open Door Note
    4. Reactions of other nations
  D. The Boxer Rebellion
  E. Success of Hay's policy
  F. Russo-Japanese War
    1. Basis for antagonism
    2. Roosevelt's efforts for peace
  G. United States relations with Japan
    1. Promises to respect each other's possessions
    2. Fears of the "yellow peril"
    3. Gentlemen's Agreement of 1907

XI. The Panama Canal
  A. Background of need for the canal
  B. Negotiations with the British and French
  C. Difficulties in negotiations with Colombia
  D. The revolution in Panama
  E. Conclusion of negotiations
  F. Construction of the canal
  G. Legacies of the incident in future relations with Latin America

XII. Development of the Roosevelt Corollary
  A. Problems of debt collection
  B. Formulation of the corollary

XIII. Taft's "Dollar Diplomacy"
  A. Uses in China

B. Loans to Latin America
C. Use of the marines in Nicaragua

XIV. Other diplomatic efforts
A. Settlement of the Alaskan Boundary

Dispute (1902)
B. Development of the Algeciras
Conference (1906)
C. Dispatch of the "Great White
Fleet" (1907–1909)

KEY ITEMS OF CHRONOLOGY

Purchase of Alaska	1867
Venezuelan Boundary Dispute submitted to arbitration	1897
de Lome letter revealed	Feb. 9, 1898
Maine sunk	Feb. 15, 1898
War formally declared between Spain and the United States	April 1898
Hawaii annexed	July 1898
Armistice	August 1898
Treaty of Paris	December 1898
Anti-Imperialist League formed	1899
Open Door Notes	1899
Panama Canal acquired	1903
Roosevelt Corollary announced	1904
Gentlemen's Agreement with Japan	1907

TERMS TO MASTER

Listed below are some important terms or people with which you should be familiar after you complete the study of this chapter. Explain the significance of each name or term.

1. William H. Seward
2. Hamilton Fish
3. Alfred Thayer Mahan
4. John Fiske
5. Josiah Strong
6. James G. Blaine
7. pelagic sealing controversy
8. Venezuelan boundary dispute
9. yellow journalism
10. de Lome letter
11. Teller Amendment
12. American Anti-Imperialist League
13. Insular Cases
14. Platt Amendment
15. Open-Door Policy
16. Boxer Rebellion
17. gentlemen's agreement
18. Roosevelt Corollary
19. dollar diplomacy

VOCABULARY BUILDING

Listed below are some words or phrases used in this chapter. Look up each word in your dictionary unless the meaning is given here.

1. caprice
2. filibustering
3. tutelary

EXERCISES FOR UNDERSTANDING

When you have completed the reading of the chapter, answer each of the following questions. If you have difficulty, go back and reread the section of the chapter related to the question.

Multiple-Choice Questions

Select the letter of the response which best completes the statement.

1. Which of the following overseas possessions of the United States was *not* acquired prior to 1898?
   A. Alaska
   B. Midway Islands
   C. Hawaiian Islands
   D. Pago Pago in the Somoan Islands

2. As a result of the Spanish-American War the United States acquired all of the following *except which one?*
   A. Puerto Rico
   B. Hawaiian Islands
   C. Guam
   D. Philippines

3. Wealthy planters in Hawaii wanted annexation by the United States to allow
   A. them to receive a bounty on all sugar produced
   B. immigration of Orientals from the islands to the United States mainland
   C. protection of the American navy against Chinese takeover
   D. access to the American market for their electrical manufacturers

4. Josiah Strong is noted for his argument that
   A. America needed a strong navy
   B. the United States needed to expand into Latin America
   C. the United States had a Christian mission to aid peoples in underdeveloped areas
   D. the closing of the frontier left us with no other route for expansion than overseas

5. According to the text, the key factor propelling the United States into the Spanish-American War was
   A. the desire of businessmen to control trade and manufacturing in Cuba
   B. the hope of missionaries to convert the Cuban people
   C. McKinley's desire to gain political support from his acquisitions
   D. the frenzy of public opinion for war

6. In the Insular Cases, the Supreme Court ruled that
   A. the American Constitution must follow the flag
   B. the United States had authority to collect debts for European nations
   C. the overseas possessions had no fundamental rights of freedom of speech, press, or religion
   D. the overseas possessions could have the full rights of Americans only if Congress specifically acted to extend those rights to them

7. Taft's "dollar diplomacy" in Asia involved
   A. extension of United States foreign aid to develop China
   B. paying the Chinese to stop their emigration to the United States
   C. United States government intervention to help American investors with their plans to finance development in China
   D. payment of other powers not to compete with the United States in Asia

8. The Panama Canal became a United States territory through
   A. a treaty with Colombia
   B. United States conquest of the area
   C. a revolution in Panama followed by a treaty with that new country
   D. annexation to the United States

True-False Questions

Indicate whether each statement is true or false.

1. James G. Blaine was secretary of state under two different presidents.
2. The Venezuelan Boundary Dispute involved a conflict over control of the river between Venezuela and Brazil.
3. More United States soldiers were killed by disease than by the enemy in the Spanish-American War.
4. The greatest battle of the

Spanish-American War took place in Manila Bay.

5. The Platt Amendment guaranteed that the United States would never annex Cuba.
6. America's Open-Door policy for China allowed unlimited immigration of Chinese to the United States.
7. In the gentlemen's agreement, Japan accepted limits on naval armaments.
8. The Roosevelt Corollary allowed the United States to collect Latin American debts for European countries.

Essay Questions

1. List and explain the major motives for imperialism in the late nineteenth century.
2. Discuss the arguments for and against

acquisition of the Philippines.
3. Trace the movement for the acquisition of Hawaii.
4. Explain the Supreme Court decision in the Insular Cases and the ramifications of that decision.
5. Account for the acquisition of the Panama Canal.
6. Explain the development of the Roosevelt Corollary.
7. Has the United States been more or less aggressive in its imperialist aspirations than have other countries?
8. How did the United States in the late nineteenth and early twentieth centuries plant the seeds of later hostility in Latin America? Should we have stayed out of Latin America and allowed other countries to develop it? What policy would you have advocated for the United States in Latin America?

DOCUMENT

McKinley's "War" Message to Congress

McKinley's message of April 11, 1898, attempted to summarize American relations with Cuba. Read it carefully to gain an understanding of his perception of events.

Obedient to that precept of the Constitution which commands the President to give from time to time to the Congress information of the state of the Union and to recommend to their consideration such measures as he shall judge necessary and expedient, it becomes my duty now to address your body with regard to the grave crisis that has arisen in the relations of the United States to Spain by reason of the warfare that for more than three years has raged in the neighboring island of Cuba. . . .

Since the present revolution began, in February, 1895, this country has seen the fertile domain at our threshold ravaged by fire and sword in the course of a struggle unequaled in the history of the island and rarely paralleled as to the numbers of the combatants and the bitterness of the contest by any revolution of modern times where a dependent people striving to be free have been opposed by the power of the sovereign state. . . .

Our trade has suffered, the capital invested by our citizens in Cuba has been largely lost, and the temper and forbearance of our people have been so sorely tried as to beget a perilous unrest among our own citizens. . . .

The agricultural population to the estimated number of 300,000 or more was herded within the towns and their immediate vicinage, deprived of the means of support, rendered destitute of shelter, left poorly clad, and exposed to the most unsanitary conditions. As the scarcity of food increased with the devastation of the depopulated areas of production, destitution and want became misery and starvation. Month by month the death rate increased in an alarming ratio. By March, 1897, according to conservative estimates from official Spanish sources, the mortality among the reconcentrados from starvation and diseases thereto incident exceeded 50 per cent of their total number. . . .

The war in Cuba is of such a nature that short of subjugation or extermination, a final military victory for either side seems impracticable. The alternative lies in the physical exhaustion of the one or the other party, or perhaps of both. . . . The prospect of such a protraction and conclusion of the present strife is a contingency hardly to be contemplated with equanimity by the civilized world, and least of all by the United States, affected and injured as we are, deeply and intimately, by its very existence. . . .

The forcible intervention of the United States as a neutral to stop the war, according to the large dictates of humanity and following many historical precedents where neighboring States have interfered to check the hopeless sacrifices of life by internecine conflicts beyond their borders, is justifiable on rational grounds. It involves, however, hostile constraint upon both the parties to the contest as well to enforce a truce as to guide the eventual settlement.

. . . The present condition of affairs in Cuba is a constant menace to our peace and entails upon this Government an enormous expense. With such a conflict waged for years in an island so near us and with which our people have such trade and business relations; when the lives and liberty of our citizens are in constant danger and their property destroyed and themselves ruined; where our trading vessels are liable to seizure and are seized at our very door by war ships of a foreign nation, the expeditions of filibustering that we are powerless to prevent altogether, and the irritating questions and entanglements thus arising—all these and others that I need not mention, with the resulting strained relations, are a constant menace to our peace and compel us to keep on a semi-war footing with a nation with which we are at peace.

These elements of danger and disorder already pointed out have been strikingly illustrated by a tragic event which has deeply and justly moved the American people. I have already transmitted to Congress the report of the naval court of inquiry on the destruction of the battle ship *Maine* in the harbor of Havana during the night of the 15th of February. The destruction of that noble vessel has filled the national heart with inexpressible horror. Two hundred and fifty-eight brave sailors and marines and two officers of our Navy, reposing in the fancied security of a friendly harbor, have been hurled to death, grief and want brought to their homes and sorrow to the nation.

The naval court of inquiry, which, it is needless to say, commands the unqualified confidence of the Government, was unanimous in its conclusion that the destruction of the *Maine* was caused by an exterior explosion—that of a submarine mine. It did not assume to place the responsibility. That remains to be fixed.

In any event the destruction of the *Maine,* by whatever exterior cause, is a patent and impressive proof of a state of things in Cuba that is intolerable. That condition is thus shown to be such that the Spanish Government can not assure safety and security to a vessel of the American Navy in the harbor of Havana on a mission of peace, and rightfully there.

In view of these facts and of these considerations I ask the Congress to authorize and empower the President to take measures to secure a full and final termination of hostilities between the Government of Spain and the people of Cuba, and to secure in the island the establishment of a stable government, capable of maintaining order and observing its international obligations, insuring peace and tranquillity and the security of its citizens as well as our own, and to use the military and naval forces of the United States as may be necessary for these purposes. . . .

The issue is now with the Congress. It is a solemn responsibility. I have exhausted every effort to relieve the intolerable condition of affairs which is at our do̅ors. . . .

Yesterday, and since the preparation of the foregoing message, official information was received by me that the latest decree of the Queen Regent of Spain directs General Blanco, in order to prepare and facilitate peace, to proclaim a suspension of hostilities, the duration and details of which have not yet been communicated to me.

This fact with every other pertinent consideration will, I am sure, have your just and careful attention in the solemn deliberations upon which you are about to enter. If this measure attains a successful result, then our aspirations as a Christian, peace-loving people will be realized. If it fails, it will be only another justification for our contemplated action.

[James D. Richardson (ed.), *A Compilation of the Messages and Papers of the Presidents, 1789–1897* (Washington, D.C.: U.S. Government Printing Office, 1899), 10: 139–50]

Questions for Reflection

Does McKinley anywhere in the message ask Congress to declare war on Spain? How could a declaration of war be justified in light of his request? How accurate was McKinley's description of developments between Cuba and the United States? Can you see any reason why Congress might have been skeptical of McKinley's claim that Spain had offered to cease hostilities in Cuba? Does this document suggest that the United States was justified in becoming involved in the Cuban matter and ultimately in the Spanish-American War?

ANSWERS TO MULTIPLE-CHOICE AND TRUE-FALSE QUESTIONS

Multiple-Choice Questions

1-C, 2-B, 3-A, 4-C, 5-D, 6-D, 7-C, 8-C

True-False Questions

1-T, 2-F, 3-T, 4-T, 5-F, 6-F, 7-F, 8-T

24

PROGRESSIVISM: ROOSEVELT, TAFT, AND WILSON

CHAPTER OBJECTIVES

After you complete the reading and study of this chapter, you should be able to:

1. Explain the nature and the goals of the progressive movement.
2. Compare the Progressive Movement with the populist movement.
3. Describe Roosevelt's brand of progressivism.
4. Account for Taft's mixed record as a progressive.
5. Describe Wilson's efforts for progressive reform.
6. Assess the impact of progressivism on American politics, society, and economy.

CHAPTER OUTLINE

I. The nature of progressivism
   A. General features
      1. Aimed against the abuses of the Gilded Age bosses
      2. More businesslike and efficient than populism
      3. A paradox of regulation of business by businessmen
      4. A diverse movement
   B. Antecedents
      1. Populism
      2. Mugwumps
      3. Socialist critiques of living and working conditions
      4. Role of the muckrakers
         a. Henry Demarest Lloyd and Jacob Riis
         b. Golden Age of Muckraking
         c. Brought popular support for reform
         d. Stronger on diagnosis than remedy
   C. The themes of progressivism
      1. Efforts to democratize government
         a. Direct primaries
         b. Initiative, referendum, recall, and other local actions
         c. Direct election of senators
      2. A focus on efficiency and good government
         a. Role of Frederick W. Taylor and scientific management
         b. Shorter ballots
         c. Equalized tax assessments and budget systems
         d. Commission and city-manager forms of city government
         e. Use of specialists in government and business
      3. Regulation of giant corporations
         a. One alternative: complete laissez-faire
         b. Socialist program of public ownership at the local level

    c. Trustbusting
    d. Acceptance and regulation of big
       business
    e. Problem of regulating the
       regulators
  4. Impulse toward social justice
    a. Use of private charities and state
       power
    b. Outlawing child labor
    c. Restricting night work and
       dangerous occupations
    d. Erratic course of the Supreme
       Court
       i. *Holden v. Hardy* (1898)
       ii. *Lochner v. New York* (1905)
       iii. *Mueller v. Oregon* (1908)
    e. Stricter building codes and
       factory inspection acts
    f. Workmen's compensation laws
    g. Pressure for prohibition
  5. Emphasis on public service functions
     of government
    a. Active promotion of direct
       services by government
    b. Development of the good-roads
       movement

II. Roosevelt's progressivism
  A. Need for his cautious role
  B. Use of executive action
  C. Focus on the need for trust regulation
    1. Opposition to sheer trustbusting
    2. *Northern Securities Case* (1904)
       used to promote the issue
    3. South Carolina speech to balance
       against the court case
  D. Executive action to support labor
    1. Basis for the UMW strike
    2. Recalcitrant attitude of
       management
    3. Roosevelt's efforts to force
       arbitration
    4. Effects of the incident
  E. Other antitrust suits
  F. Congressional action
    1. Expedition Act
    2. Department of Commerce and
       Labor
    3. Elkins Act
  G. Role of Bureau of Corporations
  H. Election of 1904
    1. Republican nomination
    2. Democratic positions and candidate

    3. Campaign and results
  I. Roosevelt's effort to pass the Hepburn
     Act
    1. Complications of passage
    2. Provisions and effects of the act
  J. Roosevelt's support of regulation of
     food and drugs
    1. Role of muckrakers: Upton Sinclair
       and others
    2. Legislation achieved
  K. Efforts for conservation
    1. Earlier movements for conservation
    2. Roosevelt's actions
  L. Selection of a successor in 1908
    1. TR's choice
    2. Democrats and Bryan
    3. Election results

III. Taft's administration
  A. Taft's background and character
  B. Campaign for tariff reform
    1. Problems in the Senate
    2. Taft's clash with the Progressive
       Republicans
    3. Reactions to the tariff
  C. Ballinger-Pinchot controversy
    1. Ballinger's actions to undo
       Roosevelt policies
    2. Roles of Pinchot and Glavis
    3. Impact of the affair
  D. Taft's role in the rebellion against
     Speaker Cannon
  E. Effects of these actions on the
     elections of 1910
  F. Roosevelt's response upon his return
     to the U.S.
    1. Initial silence
    2. Development of the New
       Nationalism
    3. Clash over the U.S. Steel suit
    4. TR enters the race
  G. Taft's achievements
    1. In conservation
    2. Mann-Elkins Act
    3. Other laws
    4. Constitutional amendments

IV. The election of 1912
  A. The Republican nomination of 1912
    1. Roosevelt's primary victories
    2. Taft's nomination
  B. Creation of the Progressive party
  C. Wilson's rise to power
    1. His background

2. His actions in New Jersey
3. His nomination
D. Focus of the campaign on the New Nationalism and the New Freedom
E. Wilson's election
F. Significance of the election of 1912
   1. High-water mark for progressivism
     a. First presidential primaries used
     b. Unique for focus on vital alternatives and for high tone
   2. Brought Democrats back into office
   3. Brought southerners into control
   4. Began to alter the Republican party toward conservatism

V. Wilsonian reform
A. Wilson's style
B. Courting of public support
C. Tariff reform
   1. Personal appearance before Congress
   2. Efforts to obtain Senate support
   3. Tariff changes in the Underwood-Simmons Act
   4. Income tax provisions
D. Banking and currency reform
   1. Work of the National Monetary Commission
   2. Compromises required
   3. Description of the Federal Reserve System
   4. Defects corrected by the new system

E. Efforts for new antitrust laws
   1. New Freedom approach
   2. Shift to Federal Trade Commission Act (September 1914)
   3. Clayton Anti-Trust Act (October 1914)
     a. Practices outlawed
     b. Provisions for labor and farm organizations
   4. Disappointments with administration of the new laws
F. The limits of Wilson's progressivism
G. Wilson's return to reform
   1. Plight of the Progressive party
   2. Appointment of Brandeis to the Supreme Court
   3. Support for land banks and long-term farm loans
   4. Other efforts for cheap rural credit
   5. Farm demonstration agents and agricultural education
   6. Federal Highways Act
   7. Labor reform legislation

VI. The limits of Progressivism
A. Acceptance of the public-service concept of the state
B. Elements of paradox
   1. Disfranchisement of southern blacks
   2. Manipulation of democratic reforms
   3. Decision-making by faceless bureaucratic experts
   4. Decline of voter participation
   5. From optimism to war

KEY ITEMS OF CHRONOLOGY

Anthracite coal strike	1902
Northern Securities Case	1904
Elkins Act	1904
Hepburn Act	1906
Pure Food and Drug Act	1906
Payne-Aldrich Tariff Act	1909
Mann-Elkins Act	1910
Underwood-Simmons Tariff Act	1913
Federal Reserve Act	1913
Federal Trade Commission Act	1914
Clayton Anti-Trust Act	1914
Sixteenth Amendment (income tax) ratified	1913
Seventeenth Amendment (direct Senate election) ratified	1913

TERMS TO MASTER

Listed below are some important terms or people with which you should be familiar after you complete the study of this chapter. Explain the significance of each name or term.

1. muckrakers
2. initiative and referendum
3. Frederick W. Taylor
4. *Northern Securities Case*
5. Anthracite coal strike
6. "stream of commerce" doctrine
7. Elkins Act
8. Hepburn Act
9. Upton Sinclair
10. Ballinger-Pinchot Controversy
11. New Nationalism
12. New Freedom
13. Federal Reserve System
14. Federal Trade Commission
15. Clayton Anti-Trust Act
16. Louis Brandeis

VOCABULARY BUILDING

Listed below are some words or phrases used in this chapter. Look up each word in your dictionary unless the meaning is given here.

1. harbingers
2. schism

EXERCISES FOR UNDERSTANDING

When you have completed the reading of the chapter, answer each of the following questions. If you have difficulty, go back and reread the section of the chapter related to the question.

Multiple-Choice Questions

Select the letter of the response which best completes the statement.

1. Which of the following was *not* one of the themes of progressivism?
   A. more democracy
   B. regulation of industry
   C. efforts to develop efficiency
   D. efforts for racial justice

2. TR placed primary emphasis on
   A. attempting to pass reform legislation in Congress
   B. executive action rather than legislation
   C. tariff reform and regulation of business
   D. public persuasion for conservation rather than use of legislation for regulation

3. TR's main contribution in the anthracite coal strike was
   A. sending troops to keep the mines open
   B. the precedent of intervention in behalf of management
   C. forcing both labor and management to talk in a labor dispute
   D. support for the concept of arbitration

4. Taft fired Pinchot because
   A. Pinchot wanted to continue TR's conservation efforts
   B. Pinchot took an administrative dispute to the public
   C. Pinchot wrongly accused Ballinger of accepting bribes to take land out of private control
   D. Taft was opposed to corruption

5. Which presidential candidate in 1912 had a program based primarily on restoring competition in the American economy?
   A. Theodore Roosevelt
   B. Taft
   C. Eugene V. Debs
   D. Wilson

6. The Federal Reserve System provides for *all but which one* of the following?
   A. rural credit by making loans on land
   B. flexible currency which can expand with need
   C. regional control rather than one national system
   D. pooling of resources from all the banks in the system

7. The Clayton Anti-Trust Act attempted to regulate trusts by

A. defining actions of unfair competition
B. placing control in a small group of regulators
C. taking control of trusts from the courts
D. repealing the Sherman Anti-Trust Act
8. Which of the following is *not* one of the paradoxical characteristics of progressivism?
A. disfranchisement of southern blacks
B. manipulation of democracy by wealthy groups
C. decision-making by faceless experts
D. increased voter participation

True-False Questions

Indicate whether each statement is true or false.

1. Progressivism appealed to an urban and middle-class constituency.
2. Upton Sinclair wrote about corruption in the United States Senate.
3. William Howard Taft was the only person to serve as both president and chief justice of the United States.
4. Taft brought more antitrust suits in four years than TR did in eight years.
5. Wilson was the first president since John Adams to speak in person to Congress.

6. The Federal Highways Act provided for federal construction and control of all interstate highways.
7. According to the text, progressivism's greatest contribution was the establishment of the public service concept of the state.
8. The Hepburn Act gave the Interstate Commerce Commission the power to set maximum rates.

Essay Questions

1. Explain the major themes of progressivism.
2. How did progressivism differ from populism?
3. What were the major accomplishments of TR's presidency?
4. What were Taft's progressive accomplishments? Why was he not considered a more progressive president?
5. What were the progressive accomplishments of Woodrow Wilson?
6. Which of the progressive presidents was most successful?
7. What were the limitations of progressivism? What lasting contributions did it make?
8. Explain the conceptions of the New Nationalism and the New Freedom.

READINGS

Two of the landmark interpretations of the Progressive Era are those of Richard Hofstadter and Gabrel Kolko. Hofstadter argued that progressivism was motivated by a status revolution, while Kolko contended that the progressive movement was strongly conservative and dominated by business leaders. Read the brief passages excerpted from the works of these authors below. In another passage, Andrew Scott takes issue with the Hofstadter thesis. Read each passage carefully looking for the central ideas presented and for elements of possible agreement and disagreement among them.

Reading 1. Hofstadter Presents the Status Revolution Theory

. . . I am concerned here with a large and strategic section of Progressive leadership, upon whose contributions the movement was politically and intellectually as well as financially dependent, and whose members did much to formulate its ideals. It is my thesis that men of this sort, who might be designated broadly as the Mugwump type, were progressives not because of economic deprivations but primarily because they were victims of an upheaval in status that took place in the United States during the closing decades of the nineteenth and the early years of the twentieth century. Progressivism, in short, was to a very considerable extent led by men who suffered from the events of their time not through a shrinkage in their means but through the changed pattern in the distribution of deference and power.

Up to about 1870 the United States was a nation with a rather broad diffusion of wealth, status, and power, in which the man of moderate means, especially in the many small communities, could command much deference and exert much influence. The small merchant or manufacturer, the distinguished lawyer, editor, or preacher, was a person of local eminence in an age in which local eminence mattered a great deal. . . .

In the post–Civil War period all this was changed. The rapid development of the big cities, the building of a great industrial plant, the construction of the railroads, the emergence of the corporation as the dominant form of enterprise, transformed the old society and revolutionized the distribution of power and prestige. . . .

The newly-rich, the grandiosely or corruptly rich, the masters of great corporations, were bypassing the men of the Mugwump type —the old gentry, the merchants of long standing, the small manufacturers, the established professional men, the civil leaders of an earlier era. In a score of cities and hundreds of towns, particularly in the East but also in the nation at large, the old-family, college-educated class that had deep ancestral roots in local communities and often owned family businesses, that had traditions of political leadership, belonged to the patriotic societies and the best clubs, staffed the governing boards of philanthropic and cultural institutions, and led the movements for civic betterment, were being overshadowed and edged aside in the making of basic political and economic decisions. In their personal careers, as in their community activities, they found themselves checked, hampered, and overridden by the agents of the new corporations, the corrupters of legislatures, the buyers of franchises, the allies of the political bosses. In this uneven struggle they found themselves limited by their own scruples, their regard for reputation, their social standing itself. . . .

[Richard Hofstadter, *The Age of Reform: From Bryan to F.D.R.* (New York: Alfred A. Knopf, 1955), pp. 135–37]

Reading 2. Andrew Scott Attacks the Hofstadter Thesis

Hofstadter presents the Progressive Era as fundamentally "genteel, proper, and safe." It was "a rather conservative sort of thing" and, especially in the Eastern states, was a "mild and judicious movement." This view is by no means shared by the present writer and it is interesting to try to discern the factors that influenced Hofstadter's judgment. He places a good deal of emphasis upon the middle-class origins of many of the leading Progressives and from this seems to conclude that the movement could not, as a consequence, have been genuinely radical.

This concern for social background and social status leads Hofstadter to his central thesis regarding the motivation of "a large and strategic section of Progressive leadership." One of the consequences of a wholesale motivational explanation of this kind . . . is that it automatically makes irrelevant anything that subjects themselves may think about their purposes. The Progressive leaders thought they were genuinely troubled by such problems as child labor, exploitation of women and children in industry, the absence of security for old-age and illness, sanitation in the food industry, and municipal corruption. But according to Hofstadter they were *really* agitating because of envy and frustration generated by the decline in deference and power allotted to them.

After serving notice on the reader that he is going to explain the behavior of a considerable portion of Progressive leadership with this thesis of a "status revolution," Hofstadter strangely makes no effort whatever to deal with the behavior of particular Progressive leaders by this means. . . . It would have been interesting to see how he would have applied his theory in dealing with the motivation of such persons as Woodrow Wilson, Theodore Roosevelt, Jane Addams, Robert La Follette, Tom Johnson, Louis Brandeis, or John Dewey, to mention but a few.

His thesis seems to be that as status deteriorates, discontent and restiveness increase. This formulation is of little value, however, unless he is prepared to argue its corollary, in which case an inverse relationship is established. It would seem that Hofstadter is not prepared to go that far, for while the involvement of the clergy in the Progressive movement is explained by a deterioration in their position, the involvement of the professors is explained by an *improvement* in their status. Apparently restiveness may increase both if status deteriorates and if it is improved—a curious situation and one that suggests that status-change alone can hardly be advanced as a sufficient explanation for the motivation of Progressive leaders.

In his determination to depict the Progressive Era as tame and conservative, Hofstadter is led along some interesting paths, such as that of arguing that the Progressives did not really favor action by the national government. . . .

The claim that the Progressives wanted to keep governmental functions at the state rather than the national level is a curious one since one of the insights commonly enunciated during the period was the error of so doing. The Progressive Platform was explicit on the point. "Up to the limit of the Constitution, and later by amendment of the Constitution, if found necessary, we advocate bringing under effective national jurisdiction those problems which have expanded beyond reach of the individual states."

The attitude of a great many Americans toward the economy was altered during the Progressive Era. The system that had seemed so efficient a means for producing the things men wanted now began to appear as wasteful and inefficient. As the conservation movement gained momentum, what had once been lauded as admirable enterprise came to be denounced as exploitation of the nation's material

resources. Unhampered competition no longer appeared benefi-
cient and self-regulating but as dangerous and self-destructive. Left
to itself, so it seemed, the economy ran wild with monopoly the
result. It began to appear that the only way to retain the competitive system at all was to abandon the principle of *Laissez faire* in
favor of a degree of regulation. If these fundamental changes in
attitude, and the demands that arose from them, are dismissed,
there can be no understanding of Progressivism.

[Andrew M. Scott, "The Progressive Era in Perspective," *The
Journal of Politics* 21 (1959): 685–89, 691]

Reading 3. Gabriel Kolko Claims Business Domination of Progressivism

Assuming that the burden of proof is ultimately on the writer, I
contend that the period from approximately 1900 until the United
States' intervention in the war, labeled the "progressive" era by
virtually all historians, was really an era of conservatism. Moreover,
the triumph of conservatism that I will describe in detail throughout this book was the result not of any impersonal, mechanistic
necessity but of the conscious needs and decisions of specific men
and institutions.

There were any number of options involving government and
economics abstractly available to national political leaders during
the period 1900–1916, and in virtually every case they chose those
solutions to problems advocated by the representatives of concerned business and financial interests. Such proposals were usually
motivated by the needs of the interested businesses, and political
intervention into the economy was frequently merely a response to
the demands of particular businessmen. In brief, conservative solutions to the emerging problems of an industrial society were almost
uniformly applied. The result was a conservative triumph in the
sense that there was an effort to preserve the basic social and economic relations essential to a capitalist society, an effort that was
frequently consciously as well as functionally conservative.

Despite the large number of mergers, and the growth in the absolute size of many corporations, the dominant tendency in the
American economy at the beginning of this century was toward
growing competition. Competition was unacceptable to many key
business and financial interests, and the merger movement was to
a large extent a reflection of voluntary, unsuccessful business efforts
to bring irresistible competitive trends under control. . . . As new
competitors sprang up, and as economic power was diffused
throughout an expanding nation, it became apparent to many important businessmen that only the national government could ration-
alize the economy. . . . Ironically, contrary to the consensus of
historians, it was not the existence of monopoly that caused the
federal government to intervene in the economy, but the lack of it.

. . . Many key businessmen articulated a conscious policy favoring
the intervention of the national government into the economy.
Because of such a policy there was a consensus on key legislation

regulating business that has been overlooked by historians. . . . Because of their positive theory of the state, key business elements managed to define the basic form and content of the major federal legislation that was enacted. They provided direction to existing opinion for regulation, but in a number of crucial cases they were the first to initiate that sentiment. . . .

In addition, business advocacy of *federal* regulation was motivated by more than a desire to stabilize industries that had moved beyond state boundaries. The needs of the economy were such, of course, as to demand federal as opposed to random state economic regulation. But a crucial factor was the bulwark which essentially conservative national regulation provided against state regulations that were either haphazard or, what is more important, far more responsible to more radical, genuinely progressive local communities. National progressivism, then, becomes the defense of business against the democratic ferment that was nascent in the states.

[Gabriel Kolko, *The Triumph of Conservatism: A Reinterpretation of American History, 1900–1916* (Chicago: Quadrangle Books, 1967; original copyright 1963), pp. 2, 4–6]

Questions for Reflection

Restate in your own words the central thesis presented by each of the three passages above. From the limited selections you have here, does Scott's criticism of Hofstadter appear to be sound? What does Scott mean by the "inverse of the status thesis"? Is his contention correct that Hofstadter must be ready to argue the inverse of the status thesis?

Is the Kolko thesis incompatible with the other two? To what extent is each of the three authors discussing a different aspect of the progressive population? How is your understanding of the progressive movement enriched by studying these three viewpoints? What important elements of progressivism noted in the textbook are not dealt with in these readings?

ANSWERS TO MULTIPLE-CHOICE AND TRUE-FALSE QUESTIONS

Multiple-Choice Questions

1-D, 2-B, 3-C, 4-B, 5-D, 6-A, 7-B, 8-D

True-False Questions

1-T, 2-F, 3-T, 4-T, 5-T, 6-F, 7-T, 8-T

25

WILSON AND THE GREAT WAR

CHAPTER OBJECTIVES

After you complete the reading and study of this chapter, you should be able to:

1. Describe Wilson's idealistic diplomacy and show the clash of ideals and reality in Mexico.
2. Explain early United States reaction to the World War.
3. Account for the entry of the United States into World War I.
4. Explain the status of civil liberties during World War I and during the Red Scare afterward.
5. Explain the process and product of peacemaking after World War I.
6. Account for the failure of the United States to ratify the peace treaty after World War I.
7. Describe the problems of reconversion from World War I to civilian life.

CHAPTER OUTLINE

I. Wilson and foreign affairs
   A. His background in diplomacy
   B. His idealism in diplomacy
   C. Bryan's "cooling-off" treaties
   D. Wilson's revocation of "dollar diplomacy" in China

   E. Intervention in Mexico
      1. Overthrow of Diaz
      2. Nonrecognition of the Huerta government
      3. Invasion at Vera Cruz
      4. Carranza's government
      5. The pursuit of Pancho Villa
   F. Problems in the Caribbean

II. World War I and the early American response
   A. Outbreak of the war
   B. Initial American response
      1. Declaration of neutrality
      2. Attitudes of hyphenated Americans
      3. Views of other American groups
      4. Effect of propaganda on Americans
   C. Extension of economic credit to the Allies
   D. Problems of neutrality
      1. Conflicts over neutral rights at sea
      2. British declaration of the North Sea war zone and other restrictions
      3. German use of submarines
      4. Sinking of the *Lusitania*
         a. American protests
         b. Bryan's resignation
         c. Revelations of German agents and saboteurs
         d. *Arabic* Pledge
      5. House's futile mediation efforts
      6. *Sussex* Pledge
   E. Debate over preparedness

1. Demands for stronger army and navy
2. Antiwar advocates
3. National Defense Act of 1916
4. Move for a stronger navy
5. Efforts to obtain revenue for preparedness

III. Election of 1916
   A. Republicans nominated
   B. Progressive party disbanded
   C. Democratic program
   D. Issues of the campaign
   E. Results of the election

IV. Steps toward war
   A. Wilson's effort to mediate
   B. Wilson's assertion of terms of peace
   C. German decision for unrestricted submarine warfare
   D. Diplomatic break with Germany
   E. Efforts to arm American merchant ships
   F. The Zimmerman Telegram
   G. The Russian Revolution

V. United States' entry into the war
   A. The sinking of American vessels
   B. Wilson's call for war
   C. An assessment of reasons for United States' entry into the war

VI. Early U.S. role in the war
   A. Limited expectations from the U.S.
   B. Two U.S. contributions to naval strategy
   C. Financial assistance to the Allies
   D. First contingents of troops

VII. Mobilizing a nation
   A. Raising the armed forces
   B. Use of "war socialism" to regulate the economy
   C. The bureaucracy of mobilization
      1. War Industries Board
      2. Committee on Public Information
      3. Other significant agencies
   D. Civil liberties in the war
      1. Popular disdain for all things German
      2. Espionage and Sedition Acts
         a. Terms of the acts
         b. Prosecutions
         c. Impact of the Acts
         d. *Schenck v. United States*

VIII. The American military role
   A. Allies on defensive through 1917

B. German offensives after Russian withdrawal
C. Instances of significant American participation in the war
D. Development of the Fourteen Points
E. Overtures toward peace
F. Terms of the armistice

IX. The fight for the peace
   A. Wilson's role
      1. Decision to attend the conference
      2. Effects of congressional elections of 1918
      3. Wilson's reception in Europe
      4. Structure of the conference
   B. Emphasis on the League of Nations
      1. Article X of the Covenant
      2. Machinery of the League
   C. Early warning from Lodge
   D. Amendments made to respond to critics at home
   E. Compromises on national self-determination
   F. The agreement for reparations
   G. Obtaining the German signature

X. Wilson's loss at home
   A. Support for the peace
   B. Opponents of the peace
   C. Lodge's reaction
   D. Wilson's speaking tour
   E. Wilson's stroke
   F. Failure of the Senate votes
   G. Formal ending of the war

XI. Conversion to peace
   A. Lack of leadership
   B. Unplanned mobilization
   C. Aspects of the economic transition
      1. Drop in farm prices
      2. Returning communications and transportation to private ownership
   D. Labor unrest
      1. Seattle General Strike
      2. Steel Strike
      3. Boston Police Strike
   E. Race riots
   F. The Red Scare
      1. Fear of radicals
      2. Bombs in the mail
      3. Deportation of aliens
      4. Evaporation of the Red Scare
      5. Legacy of the Red Scare

KEY ITEMS OF CHRONOLOGY

Huerta in power in Mexico	February 1913
Invasion of Vera Cruz	April 1914
Outbreak of World War I	August 1914
Lusitania sunk	May 1915
Arabic pledge from Germany	September 1915
Sussex pledge	April 1916
Germany resumed unrestricted submarine warfare	February 1917
United States declared war	April 1917
Creation of War Industries Board	July 1917
Armistice	November 1918
Paris Peace Conference	January-May 1919
Senate votes on treaty	November 1919 and March 1920
Red Scare	1919–1920

TERMS TO MASTER

Listed below are some important terms or people with which you should be familiar after you complete the study of this chapter. Explain the significance of each name or term.

1. Victoriano Huerta
2. Pancho Villa
3. Central Powers
4. *Lusitania*
5. *Arabic* Pledge
6. *Sussex* Pledge
7. Zimmerman Note
8. War Industries Board
9. Committee on Public Information
10. Espionage and Sedition Acts
11. *Schenck v. United States*
12. Fourteen Points
13. Big Four
14. Henry Cabot Lodge
15. reparations
16. Irreconciliables
17. Boston Police Strike
18. A. Mitchell Palmer
19. Red Scare

VOCABULARY BUILDING

Listed below are some words or phrases used in this chapter. Look up each word in your dictionary unless the meaning is given here.

1. de facto—refers to that which actually exists. *De facto* diplomatic recognition means recognition of a government which actually and effectively is in power. *De facto* recognition differs from *de jure* recognition, which is diplomatic recognition of a government by virtue of its legal claim to power. Wilson used *de jure* recognition rather than *de facto* in the case of the Huerta government, Mexico's legal, but not actual, government.
2. salient
3. polyglot

EXERCISES FOR UNDERSTANDING

When you have completed the reading of the chapter, answer each of the following questions. If you have difficulty, go back and reread the section of the chapter related to the question.

Multiple-Choice Questions

Select the letter of the response which best completes the statement.

1. Wilson's attitude toward Mexico reflected
   A. an effort to allow self-government in Mexico
   B. concern for Mexican religious feeling
   C. a desire to impose his solutions on that country
   D. fear of the power of the Mexican armies

2. Which of the following is the approximate amount the United States lent the belligerent nations before we entered World War I?
   A. $10 billion to the Allies and $5 billion to Germany
   B. $2 billion to the Allies and $27 million to Germany
   C. $10 million to the Allies and $12 billion to Germany
   D. $50 million to the Allies and $0 to Germany

3. Which of the following was *not* one of the actions that Britain took to violate our neutrality on the seas?
   A. limited us to one ship voyage to Europe per week
   B. listed food, cotton, and wood as contraband items which we would not be permitted to trade
   C. announced a plan to sink United States ships if they were found carrying contraband items to the Central Powers
   D. mined the North Sea to keep out neutral ships

4. The Revenue Act of 1916 placed most of the financial burden of preparedness on
   A. the farmers
   B. munitions manufacturers
   C. banks who lent money to foreign nations
   D. wealthy persons

5. The Zimmerman Telegram was
   A. an offer to get Mexico to enter the war on the side of the Allies
   B. a plan for Germany to attack the United States by amphibious invasion
   C. encouragement to Mexico to attack the United States in return for aid from Germany.
   D. a message indicating how weak a president Wilson was

6. The greatest power in the war period was placed in the
   A. Food Administration
   B. National War Labor Board
   C. War Industries Board
   D. Committee on Public Information

7. Which of the following was *not* one of the Fourteen Points?
   A. open diplomacy
   B. freedom of the seas
   C. reduction in armaments
   D. adjustment of colonial claims based on the need of the European nations and prior treaties

8. Which of the following was *not* a mistake which Wilson made in relation to the Paris Peace Conference?
   A. a partisan appeal for a Democratic Congress in 1918
   B. failure to take a prominent Republican in the peace delegation
   C. compromise of his principle of national self-determination
   D. too great a readiness to compromise on key parts of the treaty

True-False Questions

Indicate whether each statement is true or false.

1. Before the *Lusitania* was sunk Germany had warned Americans against traveling on it to the war zone.
2. Prior to entry into the War the United States had begun to expand its army.
3. Wilson won the election of 1916 primarily on the basis of his progressive programs.

4. The Espionage and Sedition Acts were enforced most rigidly upon Socialist and radical groups.

5. Lodge was one of the Irreconcilables in regard to the treaty.

6. Wilson's stroke made him incapable of discharging any of the duties of the presidency for the remaining eighteen months of his term.

7. After World War I the railroads remained under government control until 1945.

8. The Red Scare was directed against racist and conservative groups like the KKK.

Essay Questions

1. How would you characterize Wilson's approach to foreign affairs? What were its advantages and disadvantages?

2. Explain how Wilson's approach to Mexican affairs complicated relations with that country.

3. What was the initial United States response to World War I in Europe? How and why did American attitudes change from that initial outlook?

4. Whose violation of American neutrality was more disturbing, Britain's or Germany's? Explain.

5. What factors helped Wilson to win reelection in 1916?

6. Discuss the events from January through April 1917 which led us into war.

7. Assess the American contribution to the Allied victory in World War I.

8. Assess the concessions that Wilson made in the peace treaty. Why did he make these concessions and no others?

9. Explain why the peace treaty was finally defeated.

10. How did America's mobilization for World War I reflect progressive attitudes?

11. Account for the advent of the Red Scare after the end of World War I.

12. Characterize and discuss demobilization after World War I.

DOCUMENT

George Creel Describes the Work of the Committee on Public Information

One of the remarkable aspects of World War I was the propaganda effort launched by the U.S. government in support of the war effort. In the passages below, George Creel, director of the Committee on Public Information, describes the work of that committee.

> The Committee on Public Information was called into existence to make this fight for the "verdict of mankind," the voice created to plead the justice of America's cause before the jury of Public Opinion. The fantastic legend that associated gags and muzzles with its work may be likened only to those trees which are evolved out of the air by Hindu magicians and which rise, grow, and flourish in gay disregard of such usual necessities as roots, sap, and sustenance. *In no degree was the Committee an agency of censorship, a machinery of concealment or repression. Its emphasis throughout was on the open and the positive. At no point did it seek or exercise authorities under those war laws that limited the freedom of speech and press.* In all things, from first to last, without halt or change, it was a plain publicity proposition, a vast enterprise in salesmanship, the world's greatest adventure in advertising.
>   . . . We fought prejudice, indifference, and disaffection at home

and we fought ignorance and falsehood abroad. We strove for the maintenance of our own morale and the Allied morale by every process of stimulation; every possible expedient was employed to break through the barrage of lies that kept the people of the Central Powers in darkness and delusion; we sought the friendship and support of the neutral nations by continuous presentation of facts. . . .

There was no part of the great war machinery that we did not touch, no medium of appeal that we did not employ. The printed word, the spoken word, the motion picture, the telegraph, the cable, the wireless, the poster, the sign-board—all these were used in our campaign to make our own people and all other peoples understand the causes that compelled America to take arms. . . .

While America's summons was answered without question by the citizenship as a whole, it is to be remembered that during the three and a half years of our neutrality the land had been torn by a thousand divisive prejudices, stunned by the voices of anger and confusion, and muddled by the pull and haul of opposed interests. These were conditions that could not be permitted to endure. What we had to have was no mere surface unity, but a passionate belief in the justice of America's cause that should weld the people of the United States into one white-hot mass instinct with fraternity, devotion, courage, and deathless determination. The *war-will*, the will-to-win, of a democracy depends upon the degree to which each one of all the people of that democracy can concentrate and consecrate body and soul and spirit in the supreme effort of service and sacrifice. What had to be driven home was that all business was the nation's business, and every task a common task for a single purpose.

As swiftly as might be, there were put into pamphlet form America's reasons for entering the war, the meaning of America, the nature of our free institutions, our war aims, likewise analyses of the Prussian system, the purposes of the imperial German government, and full exposure of the enemy's misrepresentations, aggressions, and barbarities. . . .

The importance of the spoken word was not underestimated. A speaking division toured great groups like the Blue Devils, Pershing's Veterans, and the Belgians, arranged mass-meetings in the communities, conducted forty-five war conferences from coast to coast, co-ordinated the entire speaking activities of the nation, and assured consideration to the crossroads hamlet as well as to the city.

The Four Minute Men, an organization that will live in history by reason of its originality and effectiveness, commanded the volunteer services of 75,000 speakers, operating in 5,200 communities, and making a total of 755,190 speeches, every one having the carry of shrapnel.

With the aid of a volunteer staff of several hundred translators, the Committee kept in direct touch with the foreign-language press, supplying selected articles designed to combat ignorance and disaffection. It organized and directed twenty-three societies and leagues designed to appeal to certain classes and particular foreign-language groups, each body carrying a specific message of unity and enthusiasm to its section of America's adopted peoples.

It planned war exhibits for the state fairs of the United States, also a great series of interallied war expositions that brought home to our millions the exact nature of the struggle that was being waged in France. In Chicago alone two million people attended in two weeks, and in nineteen cities the receipts aggregated $1,432,261.-36.

The Committee mobilized the advertising forces of the country —press, periodical, car, and outdoor—for the patriotic campaign that gave millions of dollars' worth of free space to the national service.

It assembled the artists of America on a volunteer basis for the production of posters, window-cards, and similar material of pictorial publicity for the use of various government departments and patriotic societies. A total of 1,438 drawings was used.

It organized a bureau of information for all persons who sought direction in volunteer war-work, in acquiring knowledge of any administrative activities, or in approaching business dealings with the government. In the ten months of its existence it gave answers to eighty-six thousand requests for specific information.

It gathered together the leading novelists, essayists, and publicists of the land, and these men and women, without payment, worked faithfully in the production of brilliant, comprehensive articles that went to the press as syndicate features.

One division paid particular attention to the rural press and the platematter service. Others looked after the specialized needs of the labor press, the religious press, and the periodical press. The Division of Women's War Work prepared and issued the information of peculiar interest to the women of the United States, also aiding in the task of organizing and directing.

Through the medium of the motion picture, America's war progress, as well as the meanings and purposes of democracy, were carried to every community in the United States and to every corner of the world. "Pershing's Crusaders," "America's Answer," and "Under Four Flags" were types of feature films by which we drove home America's resources and determinations, while other pictures, showing our social and industrial life, made our free institutions vivid to foreign peoples. From the domestic showings alone, under a fair plan of distribution, the sum of $878,215 was gained, which went to support the cost of the campaigns in foreign countries where the exhibitions were necessarily free.

Another division prepared and distributed still photographs and stereopticon slides to the press and public. Over two hundred thousand of the latter were issued at cost. The division also conceived the idea of the "permit system," that opened up our military and naval activities to civilian camera men, and operated it successfully. It handled, also, the voluntary censorship of still and motion pictures in order that there might be no disclosure of information valuable to the enemy. The number of pictures reviewed averaged seven hundred a day.

For the first time in history the speeches of a national executive were given universal circulation. The official addresses of President

Wilson, setting forth the position of America, were put on the wire-less always at the very moment of their delivery, and within twenty-four hours were in every language in every country in the world. . . .

Through the press of Switzerland, Denmark, and Holland we filtered an enormous amount of truth to the German people, and from our headquarters to Paris went out a direct attack upon Hun censorship. Mortarguns, loaded with "paper bullets," and airplanes, carrying pamphlet matter, bombarded the German front, and at the time of the armistice balloons with a cruising radius of five hundred miles were ready to reach far into the Central Powers with America's message.

Reading-rooms were opened in foreign countries and furnished with American books, periodicals, and newspapers. Schools and public libraries were similarly supplied. Photographs were sent for display on easels in shop windows abroad. . . .

Before this flood of publicity the German misrepresentations were swept away in Switzerland, the Scandinavian countries, Italy, Spain, the Far East, Mexico and Central and South America. From being the most misunderstood nation, America became the most popular. . . .

In no other belligerent nation was there any such degree of cen-tralization as marked our duties. . . .

[George Creel, *How We Advertised America* (New York: Harper and Row, 1920), pp. 3–13, reprinted in *Twentieth Century America: Contemporary Documents and Opinions*, edited by John A. Gar-raty and Robert A. Divine (Boston: Little, Brown & Co., 1968), pp. 174–79]

Questions for Reflection

Why does Creel exhibit such a defensive tone in his account? Why was a propaganda effort needed to convince the American people to support the war? Discuss the ethic of a democratic government's using a propaganda effort to support its activities. Are such efforts made today? How? Are they justified?

ANSWERS TO MULTIPLE-CHOICE AND TRUE-FALSE QUESTIONS

Multiple-Choice Questions

1-C, 2-B, 3-A, 4-D, 5-C, 6-C, 7-D, 8-D

True-False Questions

1-T, 2-T, 3-F, 4-T, 5-F, 6-F, 7-F, 8-F

26

THE MODERN TEMPER

CHAPTER OBJECTIVES

After you complete the reading and study of this chapter, you should be able to:

1. Describe and account for the mood of the twenties.
2. Describe the nativist reaction in the twenties and the revival of the Ku Klux Klan, along with their consequences.
3. Describe the emergence of fundamentalism and its effects.
4. Account for the experiment in prohibition and its persistence in the face of widespread evasion of the law.
5. Describe and compare the political and social position of women and blacks in the twenties.
6. Explain the scientific basis of the moral relativism—of the decade.
7. Describe the literary flowering of the two decades and the contributions of major American novelists and poets of the era.

CHAPTER OUTLINE

1. Reaction to the war
   A. A mood of disillusionment
      1. Impact of the war
      2. Effect of diversity and change

3. Efforts to connect American nationalism with nativism, racism, and fundamentalism
   B. Nativism
      1. Sacco and Vanzetti case
      2. Efforts to restrict immigration
      3. Revival of the Ku Klux Klan
   C. Fundamentalism
      1. Emergence of fundamentalism
      2. Leaders
      3. Scopes trial
      4. Post-Dayton developments
   D. Prohibition
      1. An expression of reforming zeal
      2. Organization for the cause
      3. Crusade for a constitutional amendment
      4. Effectiveness of prohibition
      5. Its link with organized crime
      6. Al Capone
      7. Reaction to the Wickersham Report

II. The Roaring Twenties
   A. A time of cultural conflict
   B. Disdain for rural–small-town values
   C. The new morality of youth
      1. Emphasis on youth
      2. Loosened taboos
      3. Obsession with sex
      4. Aspects of persistence into the thirties
      5. Impact on family life
   D. The women's movement

1. The work for women's suffrage
   a. Alice Paul and new tactics
   b. Contributions of Carrie Chapman Catt
   c. Passage and ratification of the amendment
2. Transformation into the League of Women Voters
3. Push for an Equal Rights Amendment
4. Women in the workforce

E. The "New Negro"
   1. The "Great Migration" north
      a. Demographics
      b. Impact of the move
   2. The Harlem Renaissance
   3. Marcus Garvey and Negro Nationalism
   4. Development of the NAACP
      a. Emergence of the organization
      b. Role of Du Bois
      c. Effect of legislation
      d. The campaign against lynching
      e. Oscar De Priest: first northern black congressman
      f. Defeat of Judge Parker
   5. Blacks and the New Deal
   6. Court rulings in the thirties

III. The culture of modernism
   A. Loss of faith in progress
   B. Determinism of Freud and Marx
   C. Einstein and the theory of relativity
      1. The development of the theory
      2. Its impact on popular thinking
   D. Toward the Principle of Uncertainty
      1. The relationship of mass and energy
      2. Planck's quantum theory
      3. Heisenberg's principle of uncertainty
      4. Ramifications of the uncertainty theory
   E. Impact of Relativity and Uncertainty
      1. Denial of absolute values
      2. Assertion of relativism in cultures

F. Modernist literature
   1. Chief features
      a. Exploration of the irrational
      b. Uncertainty seen as desirable
      c. Positive view of conflict
      d. Formal manners discounted for contact with "reality"
   2. Development of artistic bohemias
   3. The armory show
   4. Emphasis on the "new" in many facets of life
   5. Role of Helen Monroe
   6. Chief American prophets of modernism
      a. Ezra Pound
      b. T. S. Eliot
      c. Gertrude Stein
   7. Expatriots
      a. F. Scott Fitzgerald
      b. Ernest Hemingway
         i. Cult of masculinity
         ii. Terse literary style

IV. Return of social significance
   A. Impact of the depression
   B. Allegiance to revolution
   C. Communist promotion of the popular front after 1935
   D. Novels of social significance
      1. John Dos Passos
      2. John Steinbeck
      3. Richard Wright
   E. The Southern Renaissance
      1. Effect of Mencken's critique of the South
      2. Emergence of the Fugitive Poets
      3. Emphasis on the values of tradition in the agrarian South
      4. Southern regionalism in society
      5. Novelists of note
         a. Thomas Wolfe
         b. William Faulkner
   F. Documentary expression in the 1930s
      1. Works of the Federal Theater Project
      2. Photographic documentation
   G. The discovery of American culture

KEY ITEMS OF CHRONOLOGY

Einstein's paper on the theory of relativity	1905
Organization of the NAACP	1910

Formation of the new Ku Klux Klan	1915
Ratification of the Eighteenth Amendment (prohibition)	1919
Ratification of the Nineteenth Amendment (women's suffrage)	1920
Scopes trial	1924
Hemingway's *The Sun Also Rises* published	1926
Execution of Sacco and Vanzetti	1927
Heisenberg's principle of uncertainty stated	1927
Fugitives' manifesto: *I'll Take My Stand*	1930
Communist party began collaboration with popular front	1935
John Steinbeck's *The Grapes of Wrath* published	1939
Richard Wright's *Native Son* published	1940

TERMS TO MASTER

Listed below are some important terms of people with which you should be familiar after you complete the study of this chapter. Explain the significance of each name or term.

1. Sacco and Vanzetti
2. KKK
3. the "Five Points"
4. "monkey trial"
5. Eighteenth Amendment
6. Great Migration
7. Marcus Garvey
8. NAACP
9. theory of relativity
10. principle of uncertainty
11. modernist movement
12. F. Scott Fitzgerald
13. Ernest Hemingway
14. John Dos Passos
15. John Steinbeck
16. Richard Wright
17. "The Sahara of the Bozart"
18. Fugitive Poets
19. Thomas Wolfe
20. William Faulkner

VOCABULARY BUILDING

Listed below are some words or phrases used in this chapter. Look up each word in your dictionary unless the meaning is given here.

1. meliorist
2. polyglot
3. ballyhoo
4. sardonic
5. bunco
6. banality
7. arcane

EXERCISES FOR UNDERSTANDING

When you have completed the reading of the chapter, answer each of the following questions. If you have difficulty, go back and reread the section of the chapter related to the question.

Multiple-Choice Questions

Select the letter of the response which best completes the statement.

1. The immigration acts of the 1920s were designed to
   A. reduce immigration from all countries except England
   B. allow immigration only from Latin America
   C. reduce immigration from southern and eastern Europe
   D. increase immigration from England and Germany

2. The Ku Klux Klan declined in popularity because

A. people became less prejudiced
B. the Klan was condemned by leading southern politicians and Christian leaders
C. of internal dissension and evidence of corruption among its officers
D. of its great success in changing laws and putting its program into practice

3. The Scopes trial resulted in
   A. conviction of the biology teacher for violating the law against instruction in evolution
   B. declaring the antievolution law unconstitutional
   C. a great victory for the concept of literal interpretation of the Bible because it was shown to be so intellectually sound during the trial
   D. the conviction of William Jennings Bryan for violation of free speech

4. Prohibition can best be seen as related to progressivism in that prohibition
   A. was opposed to all that progressivism represented
   B. was another form of control of business combinations
   C. supported the progressive goal of conservation of resources
   D. represented the zenith of control of morality, which was an important strain within progressivism.

5. An important factor in transforming the institution of marriage in modern America was
   A. the decline in consumption of alcohol brought on by prohibition
   B. the social and economic revolutions which had given family functions to other institutions such as the school and the factory
   C. the new morality of women
   D. the decline of the emphasis on romantic love

6. Marcus Garvey was a spokesman for
   A. the idea of black nationalism and black separatism
   B. the Harlem Renaissance
   C. the drive for women's suffrage
   D. vocational training for blacks

7. Heisenberg's contribution to new scientific knowledge was the notion that

A. time and space are interchangeable
B. time is an undecipherable dimension of human understanding
C. there is a limit beyond which reason cannot help us to know the laws of nature
D. the only certainty in the universe is the speed of light

8. The features of modernist literature included *all but which one* of the following:
   A. exploration of the irrational as an essential part of human nature
   B. the view of the universe as operating on unchanging and stable principles.
   C. the view that conflict was more fundamental than harmony
   D. the view that freedom from convention was more important than following tradition.

True-False Questions

Indicate whether each statement is true or false.

1. The Ku Klux Klan was directed against blacks, Jews, and Catholics.
2. Prohibition presented an ideal opportunity for organized crime because only a well-organized group could hope to provide illegally the amount of liquor desired in America.
3. The chief American prophets of modernism in literature lived in Europe.
4. Hemingway's novels are noted for their long descriptions and emphasis on philosophical reflection rather than action.
5. John Steinbeck's work treated workers and farmers in an unsympathetic fashion.
6. The Fugitives of Nashville emphasized a return to the values of a stable, agrarian, southern society.
7. The phrase "Sahara of the Bozart" referred to the foolishness of the people in the deserts of North Africa.
8. Faulkner sought to vary the usual rhetorical strategies so that new insights would take the reader by surprise.

Essay Questions

1. Was the mood of the twenties more accurately characterized by reaction, as represented by the KKK, the cult of fundamentalism, and prohibition, or by cultural transformation, as represented by the new sexual permissiveness, the New Woman, and the New Negro? Justify your answer.
2. Explain the link between prohibition and organized crime.
3. Compare the changes affecting women and blacks in the 1920s.
4. Explain the contributions of Freud, Marx, Einstein, and Heisenberg to the new mood of the twenties.
5. What were the chief features of modernist literature? Show how those features were exhibited in the works of one of the authors mentioned in the text.
6. How did the depression transform the literary outlook of the twenties into that of the thirties?
7. How is the theme of nationalism expressed in cultural developments of the 1920s and the 1930s?

DOCUMENT

Testimony about the Work of the Ku Klux Klan

These excerpts from testimony before a congressional inquiry give some insight into the work of the Ku Klux Klan.

Mr. Campbell. Mr. Wright, will you state your name to the stenographer?

Mr. Wright. C. Anderson Wright. . . . I was formerly a member of the New York klan, king kleagle, assigned as chief of staff of the invisible planet, Knights of the Air. . . .

Mr. Campbell. What were your instructions with respect to whom you should regulate and how, and how you were to serve the klan or uplift the community?

Mr. Wright. My instructions as a klansman were simply starting in and giving the Jews the dickens in New York. Their idea was this, as preached by Clarke and Hooper in my presence, with several other prospective members whom I brought up, that the Jew patronizes the Jew, if possible: therefore, we as klansmen, the only real 100 per cent Americans, will only patronize klansmen. Now, the idea was this, to simply organize everybody that was of their belief and religious belief into this order and they would practice not only moral clannishness but also practical clannishness; in other words a klansman would be compelled to buy from another klansman if possible. That was how it was explained to us by Hooper. He did not really know much about it at that time; he was simply out for the money he could make out of it, and that was also explained by Clarke. They said, "In New York City here we have all the Jews; they are controlling New York; we will get under here and when we have 10,000 members here, if we do not want a certain man to do a certain thing, if this man receives 10,000 letters or telegrams stating that he should not do this thing, he is not very apt to do it." In other words, if a member of the klan should be brought on trial before a certain judge or jury, if that judge or jury received 10,000 requests from New York to do a certain thing, they would be pretty apt to do it. That was their idea of gaining control of the courts.

Mr. Campbell. What, if anything, were you told about the wearing of the mask, or were you told it was important that you should do that.

Mr. Wright. You only wore the mask, according to imperial instructions, when you were in the klavern or klan, and then only when what they called the aliens or strangers or people to be initiated were present. Of course, in official parades it was up to the exalted cyclops. . . .

Mr. Kreider. What was the object to be accomplished, or what were the duties of the aerial service?

Mr. Wright. I will tell you what my idea is and what the ideas of the flyers of this country were. We saw that the Aero Club of America and other organizations were absolutely going out of existence: they were decaying; and we felt that we should get a fraternal order together of flyers to promote commercial aviation and give the boys a chance to fly. We are all reserve officers, or some of us are, and since we have been out of the Army we have never seen an airplane. If we take our reserve documents and go to a field to fly we are told there are no ships available, and we have to go through a certain medical examination, which is ridiculous, but we can not fly. So we got several together. . . .

Mr. Kreider. Did all the members of this organization, known as the Knights of the Air, have to be members of the Ku-Klux Klan?

Mr. Wright. No, sir, but here is where the hitch came, as decided by Clarke; he said, "No man can become an officer of the Knights of the Air who is not a klansman; we will absolutely control the Knights of the Air through having only klansmen as officers." That was the first thing; and then Clarke decided that the equipment that the klan got should be placed in his name and not in the name of the Knights of the Air, his idea being to absolutely control it with an iron hand. As I say, out there it was talked over for two days what we were going to do, and he was very visionary, and he saw Edward Young Clarke controlling the air in America, without question or belief. . . .

Mr. Kreider. Was this organization to be used later on or at any time to terrorize men?

Mr. Wright. Oh, no. The Knights of the Air was simply started into being with the flyers as something to get us together, and was capitalized by Clarke as a money-making plan; that is all. I afterwards saw letters, after I left Atlanta, being sent out under the name of Mr. Cherry, who was a klansman, and an assistant over in the office, who had never seen an airplane, I think, to all the aero clubs and flyers throughout the country, saying what a great thing the Knights of the Air was; in fact, after I left there, there was nobody that I know of that was a flyer or a reserve officer in the Army. It was simply a case of Clarke's ideas being absolutely so that no man could conscientiously go into it as a reserve officer in the United States Army. There is no question about it. The whole Ku-Klux Klan is simply based on treason against the country, in this way, that they have planned and schemed and would have, if not publicly exposed, gotten control of practically every seat of government through their tremendous voting power. In the State of Texas to-day I venture to say that practically all the smaller cities are absolutely controlled by the klan from the mayor on down. Texas should be the headquarters of the Ku-Klux Klan and not Georgia, because in Georgia they all look upon it more as a joke—the Atlanta people. . . .

Mr. Fess. What is the purpose of the parades we hear about?

Mr. Wright. The parades?

Mr. Fess. Yes; we have had statements about terrorizing.

Mr. Wright. Well, the idea is this, which I can prove and will be very glad to file before the committee, by their own semiofficial organ, the Searchlight—the idea was simply to terrorize people by showing their strength. To cite an instance of that, in Dallas, Tex., they were having trouble there with a certain class of the building trades—I do not know just exactly what it was—and the klan decided they would hold a parade to show their strength. So it seems like it was all arranged with the city authorities and the parade was held in Dallas, and they marched down the street in full regalia, and about the time they appeared the lights were all extinguished, and the next day the people were back at work. This is cited in their semiofficial organ and in the press throughout the country. . . .

Mr. Snell. What induced you to disclose the secrets of the klan?

Mr. Wright. Why did I?

Mr. Snell. Yes, anything special?

Mr. Wright. Yes, sir. My reason was simply this: I have nothing against the mass of klansmen. They go into it in ignorance, and I knew that. My idea was not to expose so much race hatred, which would drive lots of people into the klan. In other words, there are enough narrow-minded people who would be glad enough to join an order against the Jews, Catholics, foreign born, and Negroes; but if you can show a man where he was simply taken in and made a goat of in order to get money out of him by selling all these mystic contrivances and show him how his money went and the men it was making wealthy and the women who was behind the whole thing and show him where the man at the head of the order was not receiving any money or the imperial treasury was not receiving any money, I figures the klansmen should know that and would be glad to know that, whether they had done any violence or anything else. In other words, I think to-day the more the papers preach on the Ku-Klux Klan as preaching racial hatred, the more members they are going to get, because there are so many narrow-minded people who will join, but when you can show them where their money goes and what a fool he is made and the character of the people getting it, then I think the klansmen of the country will realize and wake up to what they have gone into.

[The Ku Klux Klan, Committee on Rules, House of Representatives, 67th Cong., 1st session, pp. 15–27, quoted in *Looking for America,* edited by Stanley I. Kutler, (New York: W. W. Norton, 1979), 2:352–56]

Questions for Reflection

Why does Wright say that the Klan was engaged in treason? What were the prospects for the Klan's success? How did the conditions of America in the twenties help to develop the Klan's attitudes as shown in this document?

ANSWERS TO MULTIPLE-CHOICE AND TRUE-FALSE QUESTIONS

Multiple-Choice Questions

1-C, 2-C, 3-A, 4-D, 5-B, 6-A, 7-C, 8-B

True-False Questions

1-T, 2-T, 3-T, 4-F, 5-F, 6-T, 7-F, 8-T

27 ✍

TO NORMALCY—AND BACK

CHAPTER OBJECTIVES

After you complete the reading and study of this chapter, you should be able to:

1. Describe the effects of the Harding presidency upon the nation.
2. Explain the new prosperity of the twenties.
3. Describe the features of the economy in the New Era decade.
4. Explain Hoover's policies for the nation and indicate their effects.
5. Account for the stock market crash of 1929.
6. Describe the status of farmers during the twenties.
7. Describe the status of labor unions during the 1920s.

CHAPTER OUTLINE

I. The fate of Progressivism in the twenties
   A. Causes for the dissolution of the progressive coalition in Congress
      1. Disaffection with American entry into the war and with the war's aftermath
      2. Administration's attitude toward labor
      3. Farmers' concerns about wartime price controls

4. Intellectuals' disillusionment with conservative trends like prohibition
5. Middle class preoccupied with business
   B. Survivals of Progressivism in the twenties
      1. Domination of Congress
      2. Strong pressure at local levels for "good government" and public services
      3. Reform impulse transformed into the drive for moral righteousness

II. The election of 1920
   A. Mood of the country
   B. Republican shift to the right
   C. Democratic nomination contest
   D. Nature of the campaign
   E. Results

III. The Harding administration
   A. The Harding appointments
   B. Nature of the Harding presidency
   C. Efforts for economy
   D. Deemphasis on regulating agencies
   E. Corruption in the administration
   F. Harding's death
   G. Public reaction

IV. The Coolidge years
   A. Character of the man
   B. The election of 1924
      1. Coolidge's control of the Republican party

2. Dissension among the Democrats
3. Emergence of the Progressive party
4. Results of the election
C. Aspects of the New Era
   1. Absorption of the Progressive Coalition
   2. Growth of the economy and advertising
   3. Impact of installment buying
   4. Development of the movies
   5. Growth of radio
   6. Growth of aviation
   7. Impact of the automobile
   8. Advent of mass production
     a. Impact of Ford and Flanders
     b. The development of scientific management
D. Hoover's role
   1. His concept of voluntary cooperation
   2. Growth of the Commerce Department
   3. Promotion of trade associations
   4. The acquiescence of the Supreme Court
E. Problems in agriculture
   1. Reasons for the agricultural slump
   2. Mechanization of farms
   3. New farm organizations
     a. Marketing associations
     b. American Farm Bureau Federation
     c. Formation of the Farm Bloc in Congress
   4. Legislation favorable to agriculture
     a. Early acts
     b. The McNary Haugen scheme
F. Setbacks for unions
   1. Earnings in industry
   2. Development of the "American Plan"

3. Other efforts to forestall unions
4. Attitude to the courts
5. Results of these policies
G. The election of 1928
   1. The Republican position
   2. The Democratic choice
   3. Issues of the election
   4. Results

V. The Hoover presidency
A. The prospects for success
B. Hoover's general policies
C. His support for agriculture
   1. Aids for cooperative marketing
   2. Tariff increases
D. The speculative mania
   1. The Florida real estate bubble
   2. Development of the Great Bull Market
   3. Efforts to curb the market
E. The crash
   1. Description of the crash
   2. Immediate effects
   3. Causes for the crash
F. Hoover's efforts for recovery
   1. Advocates of laissez-faire
   2. Hoover's exhortations
   3. Public works and credit
   4. Democratic victory in 1930
   5. Hoover's insistence on voluntarism
   6. International complications
G. Congressional initiatives
   1. The RFC and its role
   2. Help for financial institutions
   3. Plans for relief
H. Plight of the farmers
   1. Their plight
   2. Means of farmer protest
     a. Farmer's Holiday Association
     b. Revolutionary appeals
     c. The "Bonus Expeditionary Force"
I. Mood of the nation

KEY ITEMS OF CHRONOLOGY

Birth of a Nation first presented	1915
Station KDKA began regular broadcasts	November 1920
Fordney-McCumber Tariff	1922
Lindbergh flight	May 1927
McNary-Haugen bills passed Congress	1927, 1928

Stock market crash	October 1929
Smoot-Hawley Tariff	1930
Hoover's moratorium on war-debt payments	1931
Creation of RFC	1932
Attack on the Bonus Expeditionary Force	July 1932

TERMS TO MASTER

Listed below are some important terms or people with which you should be familiar after you complete the study of this chapter. Explain the significance of each name or term.

1. Fordney-McCumber Tariff
2. Teapot Dome Affair
3. Robert M. La Follette
4. *Birth of a Nation*
5. Charles A. Lindbergh, Jr.
6. Frederick W. Taylor
7. Bureau of Standards
8. Marketing cooperatives
9. Farm Bureau Federation
10. McNary-Haugen scheme
11. "American Plan"
12. Alfred E. Smith
13. Agricultural Marketing Act
14. Florida real estate boom
15. Reconstruction Finance Corporation
16. Federal Home Loan Bank Act
17. Bonus Expeditionary Force

VOCABULARY BUILDING

Listed below are some words or phrases used in this chapter. Look up each word in your dictionary unless the meaning is given here.

1. taciturn
2. apocryphal

EXERCISES FOR UNDERSTANDING

When you have completed the reading of the chapter, answer each of the following questions. If you have difficulty, go back and reread the section of the chapter related to the question.

Multiple-Choice Questions

Select the letter of the response which best completes the statement.

1. Progressivism survived in the 1920s in the form of
   A. the Progressive party of 1924
   B. programs for public services at the state and local level
   C. a drive for moral right and conformity
   D. all of the above

2. The Democratic candidate for vice-president in 1920 was
   A. William G. McAdoo
   B. James Cox
   C. Robert M. La Follette
   D. Franklin D. Roosevelt

3. Evidence of the push for efficiency in the Harding administration was the
   A. Teapot Dome Affair
   B. Fordney-McCumber Tariff
   C. Bureau of the Budget and the General Accounting Office
   D. agreement to allow trade associations to avoid competition

4. The Progressive party of 1924 gained its greatest support from
   A. the South
   B. big business
   C. New England
   D. farmers and labor

5. The first modern motion picture was
   A. *The Great Train Robbery*
   B. *The Jazz Singer*
   C. *Birth of a Nation*
   D. *Don Juan*

6. The "American Plan" was a program to
   A. avoid independent labor unions

B. aid farmers
C. combat the depression
D. extend foreign debts
7. Hoover's approach to recovery placed an
   emphasis on
   A. government construction of housing
   B. voluntary efforts of the people
   C. assistance to European trade
   D. government aid to the unemployed
8. The RFC provided help for
   A. banks and life insurance companies
   B. farm mortgage associations
   C. railroads
   D. all of the above

True-False Questions

Indicate whether each statement is true or false.

1. Among Harding's best qualified appointments were his secretaries of state, treasury, and agriculture.
2. During the decade of the twenties tariffs were generally increased.
3. The Teapot Dome Affair resulted in a measure to impeach the president.
4. Mass production was first perfected in the automobile industry.
5. Frederick W. Taylor sought to develop programs for the ruthless speed-up of labor.

6. One evidence of efficiency in the 1920s was in the work of the Bureau of Standards.
7. *Real* wages of labor *increased* in the debate of the 1920s.
8. Al Smith campaigned for repeal of prohibition in 1928.

Essay Questions

1. Explain the fate of progressivism in the decade of the twenties.
2. Cite evidence of the pro-business policies of the Harding administration.
3. Describe the corruption of the Harding administration and compare it with the corruption of Grant's administration.
4. List and describe the impact on the economy of each of the following: advertising, installment buying, movies, radio, and automobiles.
5. What was scientific management and how did it affect the decade?
6. What was Hoover's conception of associationism and how was it manifest in the decade?
7. What gains did Al Smith make for the Democrats in the campaign of 1928?
8. Account for the stock market crash and explain Hoover's efforts for recovery.

DOCUMENT

Senate Discussion of the Teapot Dome Scandal

The Teapot Dome Scandal came to symbolize the corruption of the Harding administration. As explained in the text, the scandal began when Secretary of the Interior Fall (a former senator from New Mexico) obtained the transfer from the Navy Department to the Interior Department of oil deposits under Teapot Rock in Wyoming. Part of the debate below focuses on the decision of Secretary of the Navy Edwin Denby to allow these lands to be transferred to the Interior Department. The secretary of the navy in the Wilson administration,

Josephus Daniels, opposed the transfer of these oil lands from navy to interior.

After the lands were transferred, Secretary Fall authorized a lease of the oil reserves to Harry Sinclair's Mammouth Oil Company. Later Fall received "loans" from Sinclair and from Edward L. Doheny, who was the beneficiary of a similar transfer and lease of oil reserves at Elk Hills.

Doheny, Sinclair, and Fall were later tried for conspiracy to defraud the government and won acquittal. Sinclair was imprisoned for contempt of Congress and tampering with a jury. Fall was eventually convicted of bribery, but delayed the start of his jail term until 1931. Fall was the first cabinet member to be imprisoned for wrongdoing committed in office.

The selection below is from Senate debates held in February 1924, while the investigation of the Teapot Dome Scandal was continuing. One of the questions at issue in the discussion is the degree to which Secretary of the Navy Denby was guilty in the matter. Another issue is the possibility that the oil under Teapot Dome could have been siphoned off by private interests holding leases to the lands adjoining Teapot Dome. Finally, there is a discussion of how much complicity President Harding had in the matter.

Involved in the discussion are Sen. Frederick Hale of Maine, a Republican and defender of the actions of Fall and Denby, and Sen. James A. Reed of Missouri, a Democrat who was naturally trying to use the incident for strong partisan advantage.

Mr. Walsh of Montana. The Senator from Arkansas [Mr. Robinson] has called attention to the reason assigned on a number of occasions by Secretary Fall for keeping the Teapot Dome lease a matter of secrecy, namely, that the contract affected the national defense and embodied military secrets; but that was not the only reason assigned. Another reason was assigned, to which, with the permission of the Senator from Missouri, I shall call attention. It is found in a letter to Secretary Denby from Secretary Fall, of date April 12, 1922. I read only the concluding paragraph, as follows:

I am particularly anxious that no details should be given out pending the final agreements upon the contracts for the construction of reservoir facilities in Hawaii.

Very sincerely yours,   Albert H. Fall

That contract—that is, the second Doheny contract—was executed on the 25th day of April, 1922, and it was obviously the purpose not to give out the Sinclair contract of April 7, 1922, until the Doheny contract, which was consummated on the 25th day of April, 1922, should also be given out; and, I assume, for the reason that it was apprehended that if information were given out concerning the Sinclair contract such a storm of public protest would have been aroused against it that it would be impossible to effect the contract with Mr. Doheny.

Mr. Reed of Missouri. That is to say, the job had to be done in secret if it were done at all.

Mr. Hale. I find in the testimony before the Appropriations Committee on May 4, 1922, which was subsequent to the Teapot Dome lease, but prior to the Doheny lease, that the Secretary of the Navy made the following statement:

That is a matter that the Department of the Interior would know about very much better than we would; but as soon as it was discovered that such was the situation I asked the Secretary of the Interior if he would undertake to handle it for the Navy thereafter, and we went to the President and secured the Executive order transferring the naval oil reserves to the Secretary of the Interior to administer in trust for the Navy, the Secretary of the Navy being a party to the policies, but not to the actual administrative work. For instance, I signed the Teapot Dome lease, agreeing that it should be opened, because we discovered that that also was being drained off.

Mr. Reed of Missouri. Do I understand that the Senator reads that for the purpose of showing why it was kept secret?

Mr. Hale. I read it for the purpose of showing that the Secretary of the Navy did refer to the Teapot Dome lease, subsequent to its making but before the Doheny lease was made.

Mr. Reed of Missouri. The Senator from Maine has succeeded in demonstrating that after it was all closed up and the goods, wares, and chattels had been packed and hauled away by the burglars some information was given out about it. He has also succeeded in showing that Mr. Denby went to the President and asked the President to turn those lands over to Fall. . . . So that he can no longer claim that he was not a party to that wrong, for it was a wrong—and I am not going to speak of it harshly, because I would not on any account say a harsh thing of the late President Harding.

Mr. Hale. If the Senator will allow me, the Secretary of the Navy also gives his reasons for going to the President and asking that the naval oil reserves be turned over to the Secretary of the Interior.

Mr. Reed of Missouri. And his reasons are no reasons at all; in fact, his reasons are reasons that are diametrically against the action taken. I do not want to be led into a degression, but while I am speaking of this, his reasons were the reasons that had been offered for 10 years by every oil magnate and every man who wanted to steal these lands. The battle had raged between the oil men on the one hand and the Navy on the other. The Navy was trying to keep these oils where they could preserve them so that they could fight America's ships in time of some great national emergency. The oil men wanted to get them so that they could make money out of them at the present time.

The contest was never hotter than during Mr. Daniel's administration in the office of the Secretary of the Navy, and it is to the eternal credit of Josephus Daniels that he stood there like a rock refusing to yield the valuable oil. I think in consonance with the advice of the officers of the Navy who knew what they were talking about, he proposed to hold them for the preservation and defense of this Republic in some great hour of peril. Mr. Doheny joined these conspirators against the welfare of the Nation, and now admits that he was one of the men who put under the President's nose to sign the paper transferring the oil lands to Albert Fall, to be by Albert Fall in turn transferred to the rogues with whom we are dealing to-day. I trust the Senator from Maine has some more evidence to read in defense.

Mr. Hale. Mr. President, I think it should be stated that the reasons given by the Secretary of the Navy for taking the action that he took were, as he states them, because—

The two tracts in California that are set aside as naval petroleum reserves, and the one in Wyoming, all have been opened by lease in order to get the oil before it passes entirely into private hands.

Mr. Reed of Missouri. Well, that could have been done by the Secretary of the Navy himself. In the name of high heaven why could not the Secretary of the Navy, as the custodian of these lands, have done exactly the thing that he pretended he wanted Albert

Fall to do? Was he so devoid of sense and of business judgment that he could not make a lease.

The Congress had imposed upon him the duty of protecting these lands; it was a legal duty; the law was plain and unequivocal. Why was he trying to turn the lands over to Fall? . . .

I have never seen Cabinet officers or any other officers hastening to give up jurisdiction. Always the movement is in the other direction; men who have power want to complete and round out their power. . . . There were oil lands outside these reserves scattered over the United States; these oil lands were set aside by the act of Congress for the use of the United States Navy when the other oils were exhausted and when, perhaps in some great war, we might find ourselves cut off from an oil supply. Accordingly they were put in the hands of that branch of the Government which would need the oils, which was interested in conserving them and interested in keeping them, so that, when necessary, we could tap these wonderful reservoirs in order to put steam under the engine boilers of our ships and drive them in the battle line and send them on to victory. Yet this representative of the Navy seeks to have the custody of these lands taken from him and given to Fall, who stands here now impaled by public opinion as having had corrupt motives and as having taken bribes. We find them, hand in hand, going to the President and inducing President Harding to sign an order that was in the teeth of the statutes of the land. There was his reason.

Mr. Hale. The Secretary of the Navy asked to have these matters put in the hands of the Secretary of the Interior because he did not have the facilities in his department to take care of them and because—

Mr. Reed of Missouri. What facilities?

Mr. Hale. And because he had confidence at that time in the Secretary of the Interior. . . .

Mr. Reed of Missouri. What facilities were necessary if the oil remained in the ground where God Almighty put it? If they just let it alone it would be kept there.

. . . If it was being drained by wells put down by private parties upon adjoining lands, the Secretary of the Interior was not a well digger any more than was the Secretary of the Navy, and the Secretary of the Navy could have let every contract that was made for putting down offset wells for protection.

Mr. Hale. . . . The Secretary of the Navy had no facilities in his department to examine into the condition of the wells, to decide what offset wells should be bored, or what oil should be disposed of, or what oil should be kept. The Interior Department did have such facilities.

Mr. Reed of Missouri. Then, why did not the Interior Department merely cooperate. Why did they transfer the lands? I will tell you why they transferred the lands—because in the Navy Department there were some great naval officers and a naval board that stood there as determined as so many lions that these oils should not be stolen from this Government, and they protested in language so vigorous to have been unusual and remarkable. They had to get away from the watchfulness of the Navy Department in order to put this roguish thing through.

Here is a significant thing. It is claimed the President was consulted all the time. If he was consulted all the time, and knew all about the matter, why was Fall's letter, so labored in its argument and so infinite in its detail, sent to him? It was doubtless to persuade the President to stand by something that the President, I believe, had never fully understood. If he did understand it, I should be sorry to learn the fact.

June 7 President Harding sent the data to the Senate with a letter of commendation, approving the policy without qualification. The last lines of this statement tie Denby into the transaction and show this full responsibility. I am sorry to add they also commit President Harding to the enterprise. But I can not make the statement without saying that I am sure that President Harding had been deceived, and that certainly he did not know of the ranch deal and cattle deal or many other deal.

But the facts adduced prove more than the guilt of Fall, of Doheny, of Sinclair, and of Denby. They indicate a lowering of official ethics and debasement of official morals. The conduct is such as would have been impossible a few years ago. At a time when we had regard for the Constitution, when we sought to preserve the independence of the coordinate branches of the Government, what President would, without authority of law, have dared to issue an Executive order transferring property of incalculable value from a department by statute charged with its conservation to another department possessing not a whit of authority to take or hold or manage the vast estate. What Secretary of the Navy would not have instantly resented such presidential interference with and humiliation of his department, and, if need be, have resigned as a protest? What Secretary of the Interior would have had the insolence to demand the possession of that properties to which he was not entitled? What Secretary of the Navy would, like a cringing coward—nay, like a slave kneeling before his master—have permitted the Secretary of the Interior to write the very orders and letters he was to sign? . . .

But again, what Secretary of the Navy and what Secretary of the Interior in the years gone by would have dared enter into a secret contract, would have dared let great public holdings without bidding and in violation of law, or would have dared or dreamed of withholding information regarding the business of their offices from Senators of the United States properly inquiring? Which of them would have conspired with freebooters to rob the people?

I repeat that the performance is only possible because there has been a lowering of the standards of official rectitude in the city of Washington. The process has been going on for years. Its development has been the occasion of many sober thoughts on the part of those who love the country and who adhere to old standards and old policies.

Dark as is the picture upon which our eyes are centered, it happily does not present a general view of public or private morals. The great mass of our people, rich and poor, are as secure in their rectitude as were our fathers. The dark spot is here in the Capitol. The people will insist, the people ought to insist, that every rogue shall be punished; that every officer who has failed in his duty shall be discharged; that every lobbyist, trickster, and crook shall be expelled from the seat of Government; and that only those who are devoted to the general weal and who will bring to it the highest attributes of heart and soul shall sit in places of responsibility and power.

[U.S. Congress, Senate, *Congressional Record*, 68th Cong., 1st sess., Feb. 7, 1924, pp. 1978–80]

Questions for Reflection

Explain the crime that was involved in Teapot Dome. Why did Hale claim that Denby had agreed to the transfer of the lands to the Interior Department? Why does Reed argue that that excuse was unbelievable? What role does Reed think that Harding played in the affair? What is the overall circumstance upon which Reed blamed the problems?

ANSWERS TO MULTIPLE-CHOICE AND TRUE-FALSE QUESTIONS

Multiple-Choice Questions

1-D, 2-D, 3-C, 4-D, 5-C, 6-A, 7-B, 8-D

True-False Questions

1-T, 2-T, 3-F, 4-T, 5-F, 6-T, 7-T, 8-T

28

FRANKLIN D. ROOSEVELT
AND THE NEW DEAL

CHAPTER OBJECTIVES

*After you complete the reading and study
of this chapter, you should be able to:*

1. Describe the character and appeal of FDR.
2. Describe the sources for New Deal
   legislation.
3. Explain the New Deal approaches to the
   problems of recovery in industry and
   agriculture.
4. Describe the criticisms made of the New
   Deal by the left and the right.
5. Describe New Deal efforts to deal with
   unemployment and welfare.
6. Assess the changes in the United States
   wrought by the New Deal.

CHAPTER OUTLINE

I. The election of 1928
  A. Republican action
  B. The Democratic race for the
    nomination
  C. The Roosevelt background and
    character
  D. The campaign contrasts
  E. Results of the election
  F. "The interregnum of despair"

II. The early New Deal
  A. Mood of the inauguration

B. The New Deal and the "analogue of
  war"
C. Action for the banking crisis
D. Efforts for economy and beer
E. Overview of the Hundred Days
F. Measures to improve financial
  institutions
  1. Extension of farm credit
  2. Help for home mortgages
  3. Action to protect banks and
    security purchases
G. Tinkering with devaluation of the
  currency
  1. Abandonment of the gold standard
  2. Establishing a price for the dollar
  3. Mass silver purchases
  4. Establishment of a new ratio of
    gold to silver
H. Relief measures
  1. Civilian Conservation Corps (CCC)
  2. Federal Emergency Relief
    Administration (FERA)
  3. Civilian Works Administration
    (CWA)

III. Recovery through regulation and
planning
  A. Aid for agriculture
    1. Wide variety of options within
      AAA
    2. Immediate action to prevent
      surpluses
    3. Creation of the Commodity Credit
      Corporation

4. Establishment of marketing quotas for cotton and tobacco
5. General effects on farm income
6. Supreme Court negates the processing tax of AAA
7. Soil Conservation Act: provisions and effects
8. Second AAA
   a. Differences from the first AAA
   b. Impact of Supreme Court action
B. Efforts for the recovery of industry
   1. Impetus for the legislation
   2. Title II: the Public Works Administration (PWA)
   3. The National Recovery Administration (NRA)
      a. Two primary aims
      b. Historical basis for the concept
      c. Nature of the NRA operation
      d. Development of the "blanket code"
      e. Objections to the NRA codes
      f. Enduring impact of the NRA
C. Regional planning: Tennessee Valley Authority (TVA)
   1. Historical basis for the concept
   2. Nature of the legislation
   3. Impact of the TVA
   4. Creation of the Rural Electrification Association (REA)

IV. Critics left and right
A. Increased support for FDR in 1934
B. Conservatives launch the American Liberty League
C. Thunder on the left
   1. Huey Long's threat
   2. Francis Townsend's program
   3. Father Coughlin's role
   4. Potential threat of the left
D. Pressure on FDR to restore competition
E. Roadblocks from the Supreme Court

V. The Second New Deal
A. Overview of the legislation
B. The Wagner Act for workers
C. Salvaging other aspects of NRA
D. The Social Security Act
   1. Old Age and Survivors' Insurance
   2. Unemployment Insurance
   3. Public Assistance Programs
E. The Works Progress Administration (WPA) for "employables"

F. Strengthened control of the banking system and public utilities
G. The Wealth Tax Act
H. Regressive impact of New Deal measures
I. Radicalism or experimentation?
J. Other right-wing criticisms of the New Deal

VI. The election of 1936
A. Republicans choose progressive Landon
B. Republican strategy
C. The new Roosevelt coalition
D. The thrust of the Roosevelt campaign
E. Results of the election

VII. Second-term developments
A. The Court-Packing Plan
   1. FDR's view of the election
   2. Effects of Court rulings
   3. The Court-Packing Plan
   4. Reactions to the plan
   5. Events blunt the plan
      a. Approval of New Deal measures
      b. Resignation of Van Devanter
      c. Death of Joe Robinson
   6. Compromise settlement
   7. Impact of the fight
B. Stirrings among labor
   1. Impetus to unionization
   2. Rise of industrial unions
   3. Intense conflict with management
      a. Techniques used by management
      b. The sitdown strike
      c. CIO victories
      d. Growing power for organized labor
C. Reaction to a new depression
   1. Course of the 1937 slump
   2. Administration's reaction
   3. The battle over spending
      a. Fear of the unbalanced budget
      b. Keynesian theory
      c. A move from regulation to antitrust action
   4. Roosevelt's call for spending
   5. Work of the Temporary National Economic Committee (TNEC)
   6. Reforms of 1937
      a. Housing legislation
      b. Assistance for rural poverty
         i. Status of farm tenants

        ii. Southern Tenant Farmers'
           Union (STFU)
       iii. Work of the Farm Security
           Administration
    7. The legislation of 1938
      a. Second AAA
      b. Food, Drug and Cosmetic Act
      c. Fair Labor Standards Act
  D. Setbacks to the New Deal
    1. Emergence of an opposition

      a. Defection of the southerners
      b. Victories of the opposition in
         1938
    2. Roosevelt's 1938 purge
    3. Results of the 1938 elections
    4. Limited legislation in 1939
VIII. Impact of the New Deal
  A. Some enduring changes
  B. A course between extremes
  C. Creation of the "broker state"

KEY ITEMS OF CHRONOLOGY

The Hundred Days	March 4–June 16, 1933
Second New Deal initiatives	1935
Court-Packing Plan presented	1937
Roosevelt's administrations	1933–April 1945

TERMS TO MASTER

Listed below are some important terms or people with which you should be familiar after you complete the study of this chapter. Explain the significance of each name or term.

1. The Hundred Days
2. Economy Act
3. Securities and Exchange Commission
4. Civilian Conservation Corps
5. Agricultural Adjustment Administration
6. *United States v. Butler*
7. Soil Conservation Act
8. Public Works Administration
9. Tennessee Valley Authority
10. Huey Long
11. *Schechter Poultry Corp. v. United States*
12. Wagner Act
13. Social Security Act
14. Court-Packing Plan
15. Fair Labor Standards Act

VOCABULARY BUILDING

Listed below are some words or phrases used in this chapter. Look up each word in your dictionary unless the meaning is given here.

1. supercilious
2. analogue
3. pyrrhic (victory)
4. fiscal
5. anachronism
6. dole

EXERCISES FOR UNDERSTANDING

When you have completed the reading of the chapter, answer each of the following questions. If you have difficulty, go back and reread the section of the chapter related to the question.

Multiple-Choice Questions

Select the letter of the response which best completes the statement.

1. The major thrust of Roosevelt's first proposals to Congress was
  A. for regulation of agriculture
  B. to give federal aid to the unemployed
  C. to achieve economy in government

D. to restore competition among
   businesses

2. The New Deal is related to World War I
   in that
   A. there was a major depression during
      the war
   B. the government had a social security
      program during the war
   C. several major New Deal programs
      were similar to World War I
      programs
   D. there were many labor strikes during
      both periods

3. Right-wing critics of the New Deal
   included
   A. Communists and Socialists
   B. John W. Davis and Al Smith
   C. Huey Long and Father Coughlin
   D. Supporters of the STFU

4. The NRA blanket code was developed
   A. to improve the production of woolen
      blankets
   B. because the legislation required it
   C. because it was taking too long to
      develop individual industry codes
   D. because the Supreme Court
      prevented individual industrial
      codes

5. The AAA was declared unconstitutional
   because
   A. it delegated too much responsibility
      to the president
   B. it did not help all farmers
   C. it interfered with farming in some
      states
   D. it required a processing tax

6. The chief threat to Roosevelt's reelection
   in 1936 was
   A. his probable failure to gain the
      Democratic nomination
   B. Republican ability to spend more
      funds on the election
   C. his failure to bring improvement to
      the unemployed
   D. Democratic votes which might be
      taken away by Huey Long

7. The Supreme Court packing plan was
   defeated because of
   A. fear that it could lead to excessive
      presidential power
   B. the change in the court's

direction in rulings on key measures
   C. the death of the Democratic Senate
      floor leader
   D. all of the above

8. Sitdown strikes involved
   A. the AFL in the building industry
   B. the CIO in the automobile industry
   C. a strike against all railroads
   D. all of the above

True-False Questions

*Indicate whether each statement is true or
false.*

1. In the New Deal, Roosevelt was from
   the first committed to a long-term
   program of deficit spending.
2. The prohibition amendment was
   repealed during the first year of the New
   Deal.
3. Roosevelt sought to reduce the gold
   content of the dollar in order to raise the
   prices of U.S. goods.
4. Under the New Deal agricultural
   programs, farmers were paid not to grow
   crops.
5. The TVA was developed from a new
   concept developed by FDR and Harry
   Hopkins.
6. The Townsend Plan was intended only
   to provide funds for retired persons.
7. Perhaps the most enduring voting
   change brought by FDR was the shift of
   the farm vote to the Democratic party.
8. Keynesianism involves reducing
   government spending in times of severe
   unemployment.

A Match of New Deal Agencies

*The New Deal period witnessed the
creation of a plethora of new government
agencies which became known as the
alphabet agencies because they were referred
to by their initials. To help you focus on
major agencies and to test your grasp of the
material, match the description or statement
on the right with the agencies or act on the
left. Some of the agencies or acts may match
with more than one description. Answers are
at the end of this chapter.*

Agency or Act	Description
1. FDIC	a. created a regional rehabilitation of a river basin
2. FERA	b. investigated the concentration of economic power in the United States
3. Economy Act	c. set minimum wages and maximum hours for certain industries in interstate commerce
4. First AAA	d. provided a variety of methods for increasing farm income
5. Civilian Conservation Corps	e. provided insurance for bank deposits
6. PWA	f. $3.3 billion for jobs on major building projects
7. TVA	g. a stopgap plan for aiding the unemployed in 1933–35
8. NRA	h. loans to rural cooperatives to run electrical lines to remote farms
9. REA	i. a plan to cut wages of veterans and federal employees
10. Wagner Act	j. jobs for young men in the nation's parks
11. Social Security Act	k. an agency to regulate the sale of stocks and bonds
12. Wealth Tax Act	l. allowed industries to collaborate together to limit production of goods and raise wages
13. SEC	m. provided farmers payments to conserve soil by not planting crops
14. TNEC	n. created a committee to oversee elections for unions
15. Farm Security Administration	o. established the welfare system for mothers and dependent children
16. Soil Conservation Act	p. greatly increased income taxes
17. Fair Labor Standards Act	q. provided a tax on incomes to ensure retirement benefits
18. WPA	r. placed a tax on farm products when first processed for market
	s. provided loans to help farm tenants buy their land

(Continued)

(Continued)

Agency or Act	Description
	t. a long-term federal program to provide jobs, including symphony, artistic, and theater projects
	u. provided states aid for work projects as well as a dole
	v. built dams to produce and sell electricity
	w. a counterpart to NRA, this agency provided jobs on major construction projects

Essay Questions

1. What special qualities did Franklin Roosevelt bring to the presidency?
2. Explain the sources of the New Deal. To what extent was Roosevelt dedicated to the concept of a New Deal when he took office? Explain.
3. Explain the New Deal approach to aiding agriculture.
4. Explain the significant New Deal programs set up to aid the unemployed.
5. How was the NRA supposed to work?
6. How was it expected to help eliminate unemployment? How successful was it?
6. How did the Supreme Court interfere with the New Deal? Why was the court-packing plan not successful?
7. How did the New Deal aid organized labor? What major new developments changed organized labor in the thirties?
8. How did the New Deal affect political coalitions and party power?
9. What is the enduring legacy of the New Deal?

DOCUMENT

The Senate Debate over Social Security

The Social Security Act was one of the most lasting and significant acts of the New Deal. The following selections from the *Congressional Record*'s transcript of the debate on the Social Security Act afford an opportunity to see what a key proponent of the act expected of it when he presented it to the Senate. We also see the explanation Huey Long gave of his Share Our Wealth Program on the floor of the Senate.

The first portion of the document includes excerpts from Pat Harrison's explanation of the Social Security Act. Harrison, from Mississippi, was chairman of the Senate Finance Committee and thus had responsibility for shepherding the Social Security Act through that chamber. In these passages he is explaining the Old Age Assistance, Aid to the Blind, and Aid to Dependent Children sections of the Social Security Act. The more familiar portion of the Social Security Act, the payroll-deduction and retirement system, is referred to here as an annuity. In addition the act provided for a federal/state program of assistance for those elderly people who would not have qualified for the traditional annuity because they would not have worked long enough to draw from that fund. It is this group to which Harrison and the other senators are referring in their remarks about Old Age Assistance and pension legislation.

Huey Long of Louisiana was one of the most colorful characters of the New Deal era. As the text points out, he was considered a major threat to Roosevelt's reelection in 1936 because with his great following in the country he had the potential to draw millions of votes which would otherwise have gone to Roosevelt. He was removed as a political threat when he was assassinated in August 1935.

In these passages Long used the debate on Social Security as an opportunity once again to present his concept of taxing the wealthy to help the less fortunate. Follow the reasoning closely as Millard Tydings of Maryland attempts to point out the illogical features of Long's plan.

[June 14, 1935]

Mr. Harrison: . . . There is yet a third group to consider, those who now or in the future face a dependent old age and have not been able to secure either of the annuities which I have just mentioned. For a complete old-age program this group must also be considered. This is the second part of the old-age security plan—providing for those whose old-age dependency cannot be eliminated by these annuities.

The social-security bill authorizes the appropriation of $49,750,-000 for 1936, and such sum as may be needed annually thereafter, to be allotted the States with approved plans, to be used in making payments under their old-age pension laws. The average pension now paid by the 33 States and 2 Territories which have already enacted these laws is about $15 per person per month. Accordingly, up to $15 a month per beneficiary the Federal Government will match whatever the States appropriate. This Federal aid will be available immediately to each State with a satisfactory plan for State old-age pensions and will result in the Federal Government bearing half the costs of paying pensions up to $30 per month per beneficiary. If the State wishes to add to its costs and pay a more liberal pension, of course it is at liberty to do so.

The necessity of the bill making this twofold attack upon destitution in old age can be readily appreciated when one realizes the terrific cost of trying to meet the problem by merely grants in aid to the States to pay gratuitous pensions. As I have stated, the number of needy old people is steadily increasing. The average length of life is getting longer; industrial civilization has made it harder for the young to care for their parents. For these reasons, if the measure merely granted aid to the States for old-age pensions, the cost would grow enormously. The actuaries say that if this was the only plan providing for the aged, by 1960 the total annual cost of pensions, to the State, Federal, and local governments, would be as much as $2,000,000,000. . . .

By inaugurating this threefold system—and this is very important—we will thus be vastly reducing the Federal and State burden of paying the gratuitous pension, for this annuity system should eliminate the necessity of a gratuitous pension in at least half the cases. . . .

It is well worth while to remember this tremendous saving to the Federal and State Governments, in considering placing on industry the graduated pay-roll tax it will assume under this uniform national system. This tax on employers, and the tax on employees, begins in 1937 with equal contributions of 1 percent, and is 2 percent in 1943. Even when it reaches its maximum of 3 percent in 1949, it will amount, on the average, to only something like 1 percent of the regular selling price of the average employers' product. This is a relatively small amount to pay for a system which will provide annuities in lieu of gratuitous pensions costing over a billion dollars a year, and will bring assurance of a small but regular income to more than half of our aged people.

Besides the saving to the Nation as a whole, the annuity system will give to the worker the satisfaction of knowing that he himself is providing for his old age.

Besides the grant in aid to States of assistance in paying pension for the needy aged—and this does not refer to one who has reached the age of 65 only, but he must be in need—the bill authorizes $3,000,000 for 1936, and such sums as may be necessary thereafter to match State funds for pensions to those totally blind. Approximately the same conditions attach to these grants in aid as attach to grants for State old-age pensions.

I now direct your attention to the second phase of the measure, that of child welfare. At the outset I desire to pay tribute to the great work the States have done in this field, and to mention that all the provisions of the bill affecting children are designed to assist the States.

The large problems relating to child welfare are the problems of the child in the broken home without adequate income, the neglected child, and the crippled child. In addition, the matter of child and maternal health is of vital importance.

The pending bill has provisions designed to alleviate each of these hazards.

With respect to the first child-welfare problem, that of the child in the broken home, where there is no adequate income. . . . This survey indicates that there are some 350,000 families of this type, with 700,000 children, which have been supported by the relief. With relief no longer available the necessity will naturally arise of throwing these children in institutions, as the mother cannot usually care for them and at the same time go out and work.

The problem of keeping such broken families together has caused 45 States to enact laws, generally termed "mothers' pensions," and with the termination of the Federal emergency relief measures it would seem almost imperative that the States be assisted in bearing the financial burden of providing these pensions.

The measure meets this situation by authorizing an appropriation of $24,750,000 for 1938, and such amounts as may be needed annually thereafter, for grants in aid, to be apportioned among the States for use in paying pensions to dependent children. Where the State has an approved plan, the Federal Government thus will bear one-third the cost of the total pension, except in no case shall the Federal share exceed $6 per month where there is one dependent child, and $4 for each additional child . . . as the contemplated total pension would amount to $18 for the first child and $12 each for any additional children in the family.

Mr. Long. ... Why, just see what is provided. Read this. This is really funny:

For the purpose of enabling each state to furnish financial assistance, as far as practical under the conditions in each State—

Listen to this:

to aged needy individuals—

Aged needy individuals, paupers, found to be paupers by the governing board of the county or State, controlled by the politicians, of whom I am one!

I am trying to keep the people out of the hands of men of my type and worse.

Think of that! Talk about appropriating the little, infinitesimal amount of $49,000,000 to pay old-age pensions to all the people in the United States who are in need of those pensions. It is the most absurd and ridiculous thing I ever heard of in my life. That will not pay for the ribbons of the typewriters it will take to mail out the envelopes to the old-age pensioners of the United States. ...

I figured out how much it would cost. Do Senators know how much it would take? It would take $3,000,000,000. ... It will take something in excess of $3,000,000,000 to pay old-age pensions to the people in the United States, who are entitled to them at the rate of $30 a month. And the proposal here is to appropriate $49,000,000.

Then where are we to get the $49,000,000? It would mean taxing the poor devil who is to get the pension. It is ridiculous! It is absolutely absurd!

I want my good friends to know I am with them heart and soul and body; I was away ahead of them in this old-age-pension matter.

Mr. Wagner. I think the Senator is confused. The $49,000,000 is for old-age assistance. That is to be paid by the taxpayers of the United States.

Mr. Long. Very well. That is the Government's part of it. It is our part.

Mr. Wagner. It is the Government's part. The other part is to be paid by the taxpayers of the States.

Mr. Long. Forty-nine million dollars is half of it, then, and the State has to put up the other $49,000,000, and that will make $98,-000,000, substantially a hundred million dollars, and we would have one hundred million when we need three billion. ...

Down in Louisiana we are honest people in our use of language. I do not mean that others are not honest in their language, but I mean we are not extravagant. We give paupers help, just as the bill before us proposes paupers' help, and the administration has been sandbagging Louisiana with these Government statistics because we will not change the word "pauper" to "pensioner." A pauper is not a pensioner.

If my friend from New York will do what he ought to do about this matter he will change the wording and say "pauper's assistance" instead of "old-age assistance," because when the language is "to aid needy individuals" it is taken out of the category of being a pension and it is made a payment to a pauper.

Mr. Long. Here is what I propose: I propose that the money with which to make all these relief payments shall be raised by tax, but that the tax shall not be levied on any except those whose wealth exceeds 100 times the average family fortune of the United States. . . .

On the first $1,700,000 no tax is to be paid. That limit is too high, but still we can make that limit. I am trying to make the limit so high that no one on earth will have a right to kick about it. It ought to be that the exemption was no more than $100,000, but we can make the limit the figure I have given, so that there shall be no tax for the purpose levied on any fortune except one which is 100 times the size of the average family fortune, and not take money away from the poor devil who is earning $500 and who actually needs $2,000 to buy food and to buy the necessities of life.

Mr. Bone. Mr. President, I did not hear all of the Senator's argument. Does he propose his tax in the form of a capital levy?

Mr. Long. Yes, sir.

Mr. Bone. I am wondering if that could be sustained under our Constitution without an amendment.

Mr. Long. Yes, sir; it can be sustained. Not only can it be sustained, but it was the basis upon which the law of the United States was founded. It was the basis of the law upon which the United States started as a Government, and the only reason why we are in this fix today is because we departed from it. According to the statement made by the Senator from New York [Mr. Wagner]—and it should have been made a thousand times more strongly—no one can question, topside nor bottom, the right of the United to levy a tax on property and to graduate the tax. Nobody can question it. There is not a doubt about it.

[June 17, 1935]

Mr. Long. . . . If they provide any more money than $49,000,000 —which, as I have previously proved, is an infinitesimal sum—if they provide any money at all for unemployment, if they provide for dependent aid for children, or any of these things for which provision is made, the States will have to levy a tax with which to do it. . . .

If the States are not only unable to levy any taxes for that purpose but if they are not even able to levy enough taxes to support their schools, if they are not able to levy enough taxes to support their hospitals, if they are not now able to levy enough taxes to take care of their own domestic affairs as they are now being handled, and if every one of the States, or nearly every one of them, is living at a rate that does not even provide for a balanced budget— . . . how can we expect the States of The American Union to levy any more taxes, and upon whom are they to levy these taxes?

Mr. Tydings. Mr. President—

The Presiding Officer (Mr. Schwellenbach in the chair). Does the Senator from Louisiana yield to the Senator from Maryland?

Mr. Long. I yield.

Mr. Tydings. I should like to ask this of the Senator from Louisiana; what will be the annual cost of administering this fund under the Senator's plan?

Mr. Long. The whole plan?

Mr. Tydings. Yes; how many billions a year would it cost?

Mr. Long. Somewhere near six billion.

Mr. Tydings. That would be in addition, of course, to the regular expenses of the Government as we now have them?

Mr. Long. No; I would judge this would eliminate about all of the present relief expenditures.

Mr. Tydings. I do not include the emergency funds. So that we would need, in round numbers, from nine to ten billion dollars a year upon which to operate the Federal Government in order to carry out the Senator's plan?

Mr. Long. Yes.

Mr. Tydings. As I understand it—and I recite my figures from memory—the national income is around fifty or sixty billion dollars a year.

Mr. Long. It was forty-two billion last year.

Mr. Tydings. From the forest, the factory, the mine, and the farm. That means, then, that the Federal Government alone would take the equivalent of one-fifth, or 20 percent, of all the earnings of everybody in the country spreading it pro rata first of all, for the purpose of the illustration. Is that correct?

Mr. Long. It would be as much as that; but it does not take the earnings, of course.

Mr. Tydings. What I am interested in at this point is ascertaining whether the Senator has figures to show how long it would be if we make a capital levy, and then another year made a capital levy, and then another year made another capital levy before the fortunes in the higher brackets, which, under the impulse of the plan as originally put out, would pay a considerable amount, would be diminished.

Mr. Long. I should say in about 8 years.

Mr. Tydings. What would be the maximum amount of money any person would be able to have, under the Senator's plan?

Mr. Long. About two and a half million dollars.

Mr. Tydings. Let me ask the Senator this question, and I am not taking issue with him. I am trying to develop his thought, because he has spoken of this several times—

Mr. Long. Several hundred times.

Mr. Tydings. And this question has always been in my mind. Suppose the Senator were wrong in assuming that more people would have $2,500,000 than he supposes would have that sum. Where would we get the revenue in case his calculation miscarried, to carry on this plan, after the capital levy had mowed down the larger fortunes?

Mr. Tydings. So that if we destroy the larger fortunes, we destroy also the incomes from those fortunes, and therefore we would have to carry the income brackets down to the man with less income in order to make up for the losses of the man with more income.

Mr. Long. That would be very fine.

Mr. Tydings. So that the man of moderate means would have to pay more income tax in order to give the Government the same return if the larger fortunes were leveled. Is that correct?

Mr. Long. . . . The beautiful thing about it is that when we cut down the size of the big fortunes, when we level down the 10 billionaires, and those with fortunes of five hundred million, and those with fortunes of one hundred million, and those with fortunes of ten million, so that the maximum fortune in this country would be from a million to $3,000,000, there will be practically no such thing as a social-relief program. We will have no such problem left, if we do as was said by the Pilgrims, as was said by the Bible, as was said in every law upon which this country was supposed to have been founded. If we will cut down these monstrous fortunes to the point where there will be only 600 people in the United States with buying capacity and allow 24,000,000 families to have buying capacity, then the social-relief problem will become nil.

[U.S. Congress, Senate, *Congressional Record*, 74th Cong., 1st sess., June 14, 17, 1935, pp. 9268–69, 9295–97, 9430–31]

QUESTIONS FOR REFLECTION

What is the size of the benefit which Harrison describes for the elderly? How might this amount vary from one state to another?

The payroll tax for supporting the annuity portion of Social Security has steadily increased since the act was passed so that in 1984 the percentage of contribution is 7 percent rather than the maximum of 3 percent mentioned by Harrison. Many claim that the system was never intended as more than a supplement to individual savings for retirement. Is that idea presented in this passage from Harrison?

What were the benefits provided in the act authorizing welfare for children? What was the motivation for this portion of the act? How was the cost to be divided between the federal and state governments?

What was Long's confusion initially about the $49 million for old-age assistance? Why was Long's proposed total sum so much larger than this amount? Who would have received the benefits from Long's plan? Where would the money have come from to pay for Long's plan? What fallacy did Tydings point out in Long's thinking about the source for taxes?

Briefly summarize your understanding of Long's plan from this passage. Develop an argument either for or against the Long plan. To whom would the plan have appealed most?

ANSWERS TO MULTIPLE-CHOICE, TRUE-FALSE, AND MATCHING QUESTIONS

Multiple-Choice Questions

1-C, 2C, 3-B, 4-C, 5-D, 6-D, 7-D, 8-B

True-False Questions

1-F, 2-T, 3-T, 4-T, 5-F, 6-T, 7-F, 8-F

Matching Questions

1-e, 2-qu, 3-i, 4-dr, 5-j, 6-fw, 7-av, 8-l, 9-h, 10-n, 11-oq, 12-p, 13-k, 14-b, 15-s, 16-m, 17-c, 18-t

29

FROM ISOLATION TO GLOBAL WAR

CHAPTER OBJECTIVES

After you complete the reading and study of this chapter, you should be able to:

1. Explain and account for the foreign policy pursued by the United States in the interwar period.
2. Describe the aggressions of Japan, Italy, and Germany in the decade of the 1930s.
3. Account for American efforts at neutrality in the face of aggression and assess its effectiveness in preventing war.
4. Describe the election of 1940.
5. Explain American support of Britain and Russia prior to the United States' entry into the war.
6. Explain and account for the effectiveness of the attack on Pearl Harbor.

CHAPTER OUTLINE

I. Postwar isolationism
   A. Evidences of isolationist sentiment
   B. Counteractions of world involvement
   C. Relations with the League
      1. Gradual involvement with social issues after 1924
      2. Repeated rejection of the World Court
   D. The war-debt tangle

1. Level of Allied war debts
2. Problems with repayment of debts
3. Linkage of debts to reparations
4. Depression and debt cancellation
   E. Efforts toward disarmament
      1. A substitute for League membership
      2. Strained Japanese-American relationships
      3. The Washington Armaments Conference
         a. Hughes's initiative
         b. Agreements made at the conference
         c. Effects of the treaties
      4. The movement to outlaw war
         a. Origins of the movement
         b. Development of the Kellogg-Briand Pact
         c. Effect of the pact
   F. The Good-Neighbor Policy
      1. Early efforts to improve relations with Latin America
      2. Protection of American rights in Mexico
      3. Hoover's moves to improve policy
         a. Ending *de jure* recognition
         b. Clark Memorandum on the Monroe Doctrine
      4. Further improvements under FDR

II. War clouds
   A. Japanese incursion in China
      1. Chinese weaknesses

2. Japanese occupation of Manchuria
3. Reactions to occupation
    a. The Stimson Doctrine
    b. League condemnation
    c. Japan's withdrawal from the League
B. Mussolini's rise to power
C. Hitler's rise to power
    1. Events leading to his control
    2. Reactions to his provocations
D. American actions
    1. Roosevelt's refusal to support the London Economic Conference
    2. Hull's Reciprocal Trade Agreements
    3. Recognition of the Soviet Union
E. Aggression in Asia and Europe
    1. Italian invasion of Ethiopia, 1935
    2. Hitler's occupation of the Rhineland, 1936
    3. Spanish Civil War, 1936
    4. Japanese invasion of China, 1937
    5. Hitler's *Anschluss* with Austria, 1938
    6. The Munich Agreement, 1938
    7. War began over Poland, 1939

III. American efforts for neutrality
A. Impact of the Nye Committee investigations
B. Walter Millis's popular view
C. Congressional effort to avoid World War I
D. The first Neutrality Act, 1935
    1. Forbade sale of arms to belligerents
    2. Travel discouraged on belligerent ships
E. Reaction to the invasion of Ethiopia
F. The second Neutrality Act forbade loans to belligerents
G. Extension of the Neutrality Act to cover civil wars
H. Further neutrality provisions
I. Reactions to Japanese action in China

1. Lack of use of neutrality laws
2. Quarantine speech
3. *Panay* incident
J. Reactions to war in Europe
    1. Change to cash-and-carry arms sales
    2. Extension of war zone
    3. Actions in the Western Hemisphere

IV. The storm in Europe
A. Hitler's *Blitzkrieg*
B. American aid to embattled Britain
    1. Growth of U.S. defense effort
    2. Sales of arms to Britain
C. Other defense measures
D. The destroyer-bases deal
E. Peacetime conscription
F. Polarization of public opinion
    1. Committee to Defend America
    2. America First Committee

V. The election of 1940
A. The choice of Willkie
B. The choice of FDR
C. Nature of the campaign
D. Results of the election

VI. The arsenal of democracy
A. The Lend-Lease program
B. Further Axis gains
C. Reaction to the invasion of the Soviet Union
D. The Atlantic Charter
E. Conflict with the Germans in the Atlantic

VII. The storm in the Pacific
A. Japanese aggression in Southeast Asia
B. Effect of Germany's invasion of Russia
C. Negotiations between Japan and the United States
D. Warlords gain control in Japan
E. Attack on Pearl Harbor
    1. Extent of U.S. foreknowledge
    2. Errors in warning
    3. Damage from the attack
    4. Other Japanese aggression in the Pacific
F. Declaration of war

KEY ITEMS OF CHRONOLOGY

Washington Disarmament Conference	1921–1922
Mussolini took power in Italy	1925

Kellogg-Briand Pact	1928
Japanese invasion of Manchuria	1931
Hitler took power in Germany	1933
London Economic Conference	1933
Italy's invasion of Ethiopia	1935
Japan's invasion of China	1937
Quarantine Speech	1937
World War II began	September 1, 1939
First peacetime draft	1940
Lend-Lease program began	1941
Fall of France	June 1940
Germany's invasion of Russia	June 1941
Japanese extend protectorate over Indochina	July 1941
Attack on Pearl Harbor	December 7, 1941

TERMS TO MASTER

Listed below are some important terms or people with which you should be familiar after you complete the study of this chapter. Explain the significance of each name or term.

1. World Court
2. Washington Armaments Conference
3. reparations
4. Five-Power Treaty
5. Good-Neighbor Policy
6. Stimson Doctrine
7. London Naval Conference
8. Cordell Hull
9. Reciprocal Trade Agreements
10. Nye Committee
11. Neutrality Acts
12. *Blitzkrieg*
13. America First Committee
14. Lend-Lease program

VOCABULARY BUILDING

Listed below are some words or phrases used in this chapter. Look up each word in your dictionary unless the meaning is given here.

1. moratorium
2. encroachments
3. fascist
4. jurisdiction

EXERCISES FOR UNDERSTANDING

When you have completed the reading of the chapter, answer each of the following questions. If you have difficulty, go back and reread the section of the chapter related to the question.

Multiple-Choice Questions

Select the letter of the response which best completes the statement.

1. America's involvement with the rest of the world was assured in the 1920s by
   A. the wordwide connections of American business
   B. American investments and loans abroad
   C. United States possessions in the Pacific
   D. all of the above

2. The ultimate basis for international credit in the 1920s was
   A. American loans to Germany
   B. German payment of reparations
   C. payments to the United States of Allied war debts
   D. payments of tariff duties in each country

3. The Five-Power Treaty
   A. made the United States a second-rate naval power
   B. stripped Japan of its navy

C. saved American taxpayers millions of dollars for building a navy

D. was not approved by the United States Senate

4. The Clark Memorandum
   A. attacked the Japanese invasion of Manchuria
   B. declared that the United States would not recognize territories gained by force
   C. stated that the Monroe Doctrine did not justify U.S. intervention in Latin America
   D. prohibited any further expansion of European territory in the Western Hemisphere

5. When Japan was condemned for the invasion of Manchuria, its response was to
   A. withdraw from the territory
   B. withdraw from membership in the League of Nations
   C. prove that Manchuria belonged to Japan
   D. take the dispute to the World Court

6. The Nye Committee investigations seemed to prove that
   A. the United States entered World War I to permit the munitions manufacturers to make greater profits
   B. the United States should back down from its dispute with Japan over China
   C. the only way to end the war was with a treaty
   D. the United States was not responsible for the success of the attack by Japan

7. When Britain became unable to purchase more goods to fight the Germans, the U.S. response was to
   A. take the conflict to the League of Nations
   B. lend the goods to Britain
   C. allow Britain to purchase the goods with cash
   D. refuse to supply more goods to Britain

8. Prior to the attack on Pearl Harbor, U.S. military authorities
   A. knew the attack would come at Pearl Harbor

B. thought the Japanese would attack in the South Pacific

C. had no reason to expect an attack from Japan

D. made every possible effort to dissuade Japan from attacking

True-False Questions

Indicate whether each statement is true or false.

1. Nations refused to stop Hitler's aggression in the mid-1930s because they felt unprepared for war.
2. The Kellogg-Briand Pact provided for multinational attacks on any nation which started a war.
3. The Munich Agreement allowed Hitler to take the Sudetenland from Czechoslovakia without firing a shot.
4. Roosevelt's refusal to support the London Economic Conference led to European default on war debts.
5. The United States tried to avoid World War II by outlawing the supposed causes of World War I.
6. Roosevelt did not permit aid from the U.S. to China in its war with Japan after 1937 because of the Neutrality Acts which forbade such aid.
7. Wendel Willkie supported aid to the Allies.
8. The United States avoided open conflict with Germany before our entry into World War II.

Essay Questions

1. Would it be accurate to describe the United States as isolationist in the 1920s? Explain your answer.
2. Assess the effectiveness of the Washington Armaments Conference and the Kellogg-Briand Pact.
3. Describe American efforts to improve relations with Latin America from 1921 through 1940.
4. How did the United States and the Allied nations react to Axis aggressions in the 1930s? Why?
5. Account for the United States' desire for neutrality in the 1930s.

6. Why did the United States' attitude change with regard to greater support of Britain after 1939?

7. Account for the attack on Pearl Harbor in 1941 and assess its consequences.

DOCUMENTS

Document 1. The Kellogg-Briand Peace Pact to Outlaw War

In the heady idealism of the twenties the major nations of the world agreed to join in a pact in which they formally outlawed war as a means of solving disputes. Joining in this initial agreement were the United States, Belgium, France, the British Empire, Italy, Japan, Poland, and Czechoslovakia. In the key enactment clauses of the treaty excerpted below, look for the promises the nations made to each other.

Treaty between the United States and Other Powers, Signed at Paris, August 27, 1928

Deeply sensible of their solemn duty to promote the welfare of mankind;

Persuaded that the time has come when a frank renunciation of war as an instrument of national policy should be made to the end that the peaceful and friendly relations now existing between their peoples may be perpetuated;

Convinced that all changes in their relations with one another should be sought only by pacific means and be the result of a peaceful and orderly process, and that any signatory Power which shall hereafter seek to promote its national interests by resort to war should be denied the benefits furnished by this Treaty; . . .

. . . have agreed upon the following articles;

Article I

The High Contracting Parties solemnly declare in the names of their respective peoples that they condemn recourse to war for the solution of international controversies, and renounce it as an instrument of national policy in their relations with one another.

Article II

The High Contracting Parties agree that the settlement or solution of all disputes or conflicts of whatever nature or of whatever origin they may be, which may arise among them, shall never be sought except by pacific means.

[*Foreign Relations of the United States, 1928* (Washington, D.C.: U.S. Government Printing Office, 1942), 1:154–56]

Document 2. Roosevelt's Quarantine Speech, 1937

In the wake of the rearmament of Germany, the Italian invasion of Ethiopia, the Spanish Civil War, and finally the Japanese invasion of China, Roosevelt visited Chicago, the heart of isolationist sentiment in America, to make what has generally been dubbed his Quarantine Speech. Look carefully in the following excerpts for the promises or pledges which the president sought to exact on the issues of peace and war.

Address by President Franklin D. Roosevelt, Chicago,
Illinois, October 5, 1937

I am glad to come once again to Chicago and especially to have the opportunity of taking part in the dedication of this important project of civic betterment. . . .

Without a declaration of war and without warning or justification of any kind, civilians, including women and children, are being ruthlessly murdered with bombs from the air. In times of so-called peace ships are being attacked and sunk by submarines without cause or notice. Nations are fomenting and taking sides in civil warfare in nations that have never done them any harm. Nations claiming freedom for themselves deny it to others. . . .

The peace-loving nations must make a concerted effort in opposition to those violations of treaties and those ignorings of humane instincts which today are creating a state of international anarchy and instability from which there is no escape through mere isolation or neutrality. . . .

There is a solidarity and interdependence about the modern world, both technically and morally, which makes it impossible for any nation completely to isolate itself from economic and political upheavals in the rest of the world, specially when such upheavals appear to be spreading and not declining.

It seems to be unfortunately true that the epidemic of world lawlessness is spreading.

When an epidemic of physical disease starts to spread, the community approves and joins in a quarantine of the patients in order to protect the health of the community against the spread of the disease.

War is a contagion, whether it be declared or undeclared. It can engulf states and peoples remote from the original scene of hostilities. . . . We are adopting such measures as will minimize our risk of involvement, but we cannot have complete protection in a world of disorder in which confidence and security have broken down.

If civilization is to survive the principles of the Prince of Peace must be restored. Shattered trust between nations must be revived.

Most important of all, the will for peace on the part of peace-loving nations must express itself to the end that nations that may be tempted to violate their agreements and the rights of others will desist from such a cause. There must be positive endeavors to preserve peace.

America hates war. America hopes for peace. Therefore, America actively engages in the search for peace.

[U.S. Department of State, *Peace and War: United States Foreign Policy, 1931–1941* (Washington, D.C.: U.S. Government Printing Office, 1943), pp. 384–87]

Questions for Reflection

What pledges did the nations make in the peace pact? What sanctions were specified if a nation violated the pledges? How was the pact to be enforced? What are the consequences of a peace pact like this one? What actions did Roosevelt ask of the

United States or other powers in his Quarantine Speech? What actions *seemed* to be *implied?* Why do you think this speech caused a great outcry of opposition from those groups who did not want the United States to become involved in the affairs of other nations? What do you think Roosevelt hoped to gain by the speech? Do you see any ways in which the speech relates to the Kellogg-Briand Pact quoted above? How is the approach to foreign affairs indicated in these two documents different from the approach used today insofar as you know? Which approach appears to be better? more effective?

ANSWERS TO MULTIPLE-CHOICE AND TRUE-FALSE QUESTIONS

Multiple-Choice Questions

1-D, 2-A, 3-C, 4-C, 5-B, 6-A, 7-B, 8-B

True-False Questions

1-T, 2-F, 3-T, 4-T, 5-T, 6-F, 7-T, 8-F

30

THE WORLD AT WAR

CHAPTER OBJECTIVES

After you complete the reading and study of this chapter, you should be able to:

1. Describe the major military strategies in both the European and Pacific Theaters.
2. Explain the problems relating to mobilization and financing of the war.
3. Describe the impact of the war on the economy.
4. Describe the impact of the war on women, blacks, and Japanese-Americans.
5. Explain the decisions made at the Yalta Conference.
6. Account for the decision to use the atomic bomb and discuss its consequences.

CHAPTER OUTLINE

I. America's early battles
   A. Retreat in the Pacific
      1. Collapse along the Pacific
      2. Surrender of the Philippines
      3. Japanese strategy
      4. American harassment
      5. Battle of the Coral Sea (May 1942)
   B. Midway: a turning point
   C. Early setbacks in the Atlantic

1. Devastation from German submarines
2. Strategy of small patrol vessels

II. Mobilization at home
   A. Mobilization of the armed forces
   B. Economic conversion to war
      1. Prewar planning
      2. War Production Board
      3. Role of the Reconstruction Finance Corporation
      4. Methods of supplying strategic materials
   C. Financing the war
      1. Roosevelt's effort to raise taxes
      2. Congressional reaction to taxation
      3. Sale of bonds
   D. Impact of the war on the economy
      1. Impact on personal incomes
      2. Efforts to control prices
      3. Efforts to control wages and farm prices
      4. Seizure of industries
   E. Social effects of the war on women
      1. Women in the civilian workforce and the military
      2. Changing attitudes toward sex roles
   F. Social effects of the war on blacks
      1. Problems of the segregated armed forces
      2. Role of blacks in war industries
         a. The March on Washington Movement
         b. Impact of the black militancy

3. Challenges to other forms of
discrimination
4. Militant white counterreaction
G. Impact of the war on
Japanese-Americans
1. General record of the war on civil
liberties
2. Internment of the Nisei
H. Evidences of domestic conservatism
1. Congressional elections of 1942
2. Abolition of New Deal agencies
3. Actions against labor
I. Congressional reaction to the war

III. The war in Europe
A. Basis for moving against Germany
first
B. Aspects of joint conduct of the war
C. The formulation of the decision for
the North African invasion
D. The North Africa campaign
1. Eisenhower's landing
2. Darlan's role
3. German surrender
E. Agreements at Casablanca
F. The battle of the Atlantic
1. Techniques for fighting submarines
2. Impact on the battle
G. Sicily and Italy
1. Invasion of Siciliy
2. Italian surrender
3. German control of northern Italy
4. The battle for Rome
H. Strategic bombing of Europe
1. British and American cooperation
2. Impact of the bombing
I. Decisions of the Teheran Conference
J. The D-Day Invasion
1. Development and implementation
of the invasion
2. German reaction
3. Invasion of the French
Mediterranean coast

4. Slowing momentum of the drive on
Germany
IV. The war in the Pacific
A. Guadalcanal offensive
B. MacArthur's sweep up the West
Pacific
1. Approval for the MacArthur plan
2. The technique of "leapfrogging"
3. The MacArthur sweep
C. Nimitz's moves in the Central Pacific
D. The naval battle of Leyte Gulf
V. The election of 1944
A. Republican strategy
B. Democratic vice-presidential choice
C. Campaign and results
VI. Closing on Germany
A. The German counteroffensive
B. Final Russian offensive
C. Allied moves
VII. The Yalta Conference
A. Nature of the decisions
B. Call for a United Nations
C. Occupation of Germany
D. Decisions about eastern Europe
E. An assessment of the Yalta decisions
VIII. Collapse of the Third Reich
A. Roosevelt's death
B. Collapse of Germany
C. Discovery of the Nazi Holocaust
IX. The grinding war in the Pacific
A. Japanese resistance in the Philippines
B. Occupation of Iwo Jima and Okinawa
C. Impact of these victories on the
conduct of the war
X. The atomic bomb
A. Development of the bomb
B. The decision to use the bomb
C. Effect of dropping two bombs
D. Negotiation for surrender
XI. The final ledger of the war
A. Estimates of death and destruction
B. Impact on the U.S. and the USSR

KEY ITEMS OF CHRONOLOGY

Battle of Midway	June 1942
American troops invade North Africa	November 1942
Imposition of payroll tax deduction	1943

Casablanca Conference	January 1943
Teheran Conference	November–
	December 1943
D-Day Invasion	June 6, 1944
Yalta Conference	February 1945
Roosevelt's death and Truman's accession	April 12, 1945
V-E Day	May 8, 1945
Potsdam Conference	July 1945
Atomic bomb dropped on Hiroshima	Aug. 6, 1945
Japan's surrender	Sept. 2, 1945

TERMS TO MASTER

Listed below are some important terms or people with which you should be familiar after you complete the study of this chapter. Explain the significance of each name or term.

1. War Production Board
2. Office of Price Administration
3. Revenue Act of 1942
4. Little Steel Formula
5. Office of Economic Stabilization
6. Gen. Dwight D. Eisenhower
7. Operation "Overlord"
8. "leapfrogging"
9. Battle of Leyte Gulf
10. Yalta Conference
11. Nazi Holocaust
12. Hiroshima

VOCABULARY BUILDING

Listed below are some words or phrases used in this chapter. Look up each word in your dictionary unless the meaning is given here.

1. dubious
2. plasma
3. plebiscite

EXERCISES FOR UNDERSTANDING

When you have completed the reading of the chapter, answer each of the following questions. If you have difficulty, go back and reread the section of the chapter related to the question.

Multiple-Choice Questions

Select the letter of the response which best completes the statement.

1. The Battle of Midway was a turning point in the Battle of the Pacific in that the battle
   A. stopped the eastward advance of the Japanese
   B. destroyed most of what was left of the American fleet after Pearl Harbor
   C. destroyed the Japanese fleet so that they were unable to pursue naval war after this
   D. placed the United States air force close enough to the mainland of Japan to carry out bombing raids there

2. During World War II strategic materials were reserved for military purposes by
   A. buying up the entire supply of these materials
   B. forbidding civilian consumption of strategic items
   C. rationing such key items as rubber and gasoline to the civilian population
   D. capturing supplies of these goods in colonies of the enemy nations

3. During World War II the wealthiest group of people in the United States
   A. increased their share of the nation's wealth
   B. were exempted from taxes if they would purchase war bonds

C. did not experience any significant change in their share of the income
D. saw their share of the nation's income decline significantly

4. Civil liberties in World War II
   A. were generally protected much better than during World War I
   B. continued to be afforded such groups as the German-Americans and Italian-Americans
   C. were most flagrantly disregarded in the internment of the Japanese-Americans
   D. are correctly described by *all of the above*

5. The first major land attack by the Americans against the Germans came in
   A. northern Italy
   B. northern France with the D-Day invasion
   C. northern Germany after the amphibious landing there
   D. northern Africa

6. One of the reasons the war against Germany continued for so long was because
   A. the Russians did not fight hard on the Eastern Front
   B. the Allies had decided at Casablanca to demand Germany's unconditional surrender
   C. the Americans and British were too timid to start a second front
   D. the Germans believed that they were fighting for the sacred honor of their emperor, Hitler

7. The repeated Allied bombing raids against Germany
   A. destroyed the morale of the civilian population but did not affect the military
   B. significantly reduced the German productive capacity
   C. had so little effect on production in Germany that production actually increased until the final few weeks of the war
   D. primarily encouraged the Germans to use Jews as war workers so they would be killed by the bombs

8. Which of the following was *not* one of the decisions made at the Yalta Conference?
   A. Russia would have three votes in the U.N. General Assembly.
   B. Russia would have an occupation zone in the nonindustrialized area of East Germany as well as in part of Berlin.
   C. Free elections would be held in Poland to select a government.
   D. Both Russia and the United States would reduce their armaments by half after the war ended.

True-False Questions

Indicate whether each statement is true or false.

1. More of the financial burden of World War II was paid for by taxes than had been true for the Civil War or World War I.
2. Blacks were integrated into the armed forces in every branch during World War II.
3. Inflation was partially controlled during World War II by setting ceiling prices on the retail sale of most goods.
4. After the Italians agreed to surrender in 1943, the Germans occupied northern Italy and continued to fight against the Allies there.
5. The largest naval engagement in history was the Battle of Midway.
6. The major matter of dispute in the Democratic convention of 1944 was the selection of a vice-presidential nominee.
7. The practice of "leapfrogging" meant to bypass some Japanese strongholds in the Pacific and leave them to wither because they were cut off from reinforcements and supplies.
8. The greatest losses in World War II among the Allies were suffered by the Soviet Union.

Essay Questions

1. Outline America's major strategy in the war against both Germany and Japan.

Explain why this strategy was chosen.
2. What major effects did the war have on America's economy and society?
3. Explain the major decisions made at Casablanca, Teheran, and Yalta.
4. Would you have agreed with the

decision to drop the atomic bomb on Hiroshima? Why or why not?
5. Russia continually called for a second front in Europe but the United States refused to oblige them until June 1944. Why?

DOCUMENT

The Effects of the Atomic Bomb on Hiroshima

The United States military conducted extensive investigations of the effects the atomic bomb had on the populations of Hiroshima and Nagasaki. Excerpted here are selections from that survey. Note the physical destruction, the human casualties, and the effects on morale wrought by the bomb.

A single atomic bomb, the first weapon of its type ever used against a target, exploded over the city of Hiroshima at 0815 on the morning of 6 August 1945. Most of the industrial workers had already reported to work, but many workers were enroute and nearly all the school children and some industrial employees were at work in the open on the program of building removal to provide firebreaks and disperse valuables to the country. The attack came 45 minutes after the "all clear" had been sounded from a previous alert. Because of the lack of warning and the populace's indifference to small groups of planes, the explosion came as an almost complete surprise, and the people had not taken shelter. Many were caught in the open, and most of the rest in flimsily constructed homes or commercial establishments.

The bomb exploded slightly northwest of the center of the city. Because of this accuracy and the flat terrain and circular shape of the city, Hiroshima was uniformly and extensively devastated. Practically the entire densely or moderately built-up portion of the city was leveled by blast and swept by fire. A "fire-storm," a phenomenon which has occurred infrequently in other conflagrations, developed in Hiroshima: fires springing up almost simultaneously over the wide flat area around the center of the city drew in air from all directions. The inrush of air easily overcame the natural ground wind, which had a velocity of only about 5 miles per hour. The "fire-wind" attained a maximum velocity of 30 to 40 miles per hour 2 to 3 hours after the explosion. The "fire-wind" and the symmetry of the built-up center of the city gave a roughly circular shape to the 4.4 square miles which were almost completely burned out.

The surprise, the collapse of many buildings, and the conflagration contributed to an unprecedented casualty rate. Seventy to eighty thousand people were killed, or missing and presumed dead, and an equal number were injured. The magnitude of casualties is set in relief by a comparison with the Tokyo fire raid of 9–10 March 1945, in which, though nearly 16 square miles were destroyed, the number killed was no larger, and fewer people were injured.

The impact of the atomic bomb shattered the normal fabric of community life and disrupted the organizations for handling the disaster. In the 30 percent of the population killed and the additional 30 percent seriously injured were included corresponding proportions of the civil authorities and rescue groups. A mass flight from the city took place, as persons sought safety from the conflagration and a place for shelter and food. Within 24 hours, however, people were streaming back by the thousands in search of relatives and friends and to determine the extent of their property loss. Road blocks had to be set up along all routes leading into the city, to keep curious and unauthorized people out. The bulk of the dehoused population found refuge in the surrounding countryside; within the city the food supply was short and shelter virtually nonexistent. . . .

The status of medical facilities and personnel dramatically illustrates the difficulties facing authorities. Of more than 200 doctors in Hiroshima before the attack, over 90 percent were casualties and only about 30 physicians were able to perform their normal duties a month after the raid. Out of 1,780 nurses, 1,654 were killed or injured. Though some stocks of supplies had been dispersed, many were destroyed. Only three out of 45 civilian hospitals could be used, and two large Army hospitals were rendered unusable. Those within 3,000 feet of ground zero were totally destroyed, and the mortality rate of the occupants was practically 100 percent.

1. *Casualties.*—The most striking result of the atomic bombs was the great numbers of casualties. The exact number of dead and injured will never be known because of the confusion after the explosions. Persons unaccounted for might have been burned beyond recognition in the falling buildings, disposed of in one of the mass cremations of the first week of recovery, or driven out of the city to die or recover without any record remaining. No sure count of even the preraid populations existed. . . . In this uncertain situation, etimates of casualties have generally ranged between 100,000 and 180,000 for Hiroshima, and between 50,000 and 100,000 for Nagasaki. The Survey believes the dead at Hiroshima to have been between 70,000 and 80,000, with an equal number injured; at Nagasaki over 35,000 dead and somewhat more than that injured seems the most plausible estimate.

Most of the immediate casualties did not differ from those caused by incendiary or high-explosive raids. The outstanding difference was the presence of radiation effects, which became unmistakable about a week after the bombing. At the time of impact, however, the causes of death and injury were flash burns, secondary effects of blast and falling debris, and burns from blazing buildings. . . .

The seriousness of . . . radiation effects may be measured by the fact that 95 percent of the traced survivors of the immediate explosion who were within 3,000 feet suffered from radiation disease. . . .

. . . Some of the dead were said by survivors to have had their abdomens ruptured and intestines protruding; others were reported to have protruding eyes and tongues, and to have looked as if they had drowned. Thorough check by Allied investigators discredited these stories as evidence of direct blast effects; the normal effects of blast are internal hemorrhage and crushing. These external signs point to injuries from debris rather than blast.

Injuries produced by falling and flying debris were much more numerous, and naturally increased in number and seriousness nearer the center of the affected area. . . .

There is no doubt that the bomb was the most important influence among the people of these areas in making them think that defeat was inevitable. . . .

Admiration for the bomb was more frequently expressed than anger. Over one-fourth of the people in the target cities and surrounding area said they were impressed by its power and by the scientific skill which underlay its discovery and production.

. . . The two raids were all-Japan events and were intended so: The Allied Powers were trying to break the fighting spirit of the Japanese people and their leaders, not just of the residents of Hiroshima and Nagasaki. . . .

The reactions found in the bombed cities appeared in the country as a whole—fear and terror, anger and hatred against the users, admiration for the scientific achievement—though in each case with less intensity.

[The United States Strategic Bombing Survey, *The Effects of Atomic Bombs on Hiroshima and Nagasaki* (Washington, D.C.: U.S. Government Printing Office, 1946), pp. 3, 6, 15, 17–18, 21]

Questions for Reflection

How do you react to reading about the physical and human destruction wrought by the bomb? How do the reactions of the Japanese people to the impact of the bomb compare with what you would have expected their reactions to have been? How would you compare the use of the atomic bomb to the use of conventional weapons in war? What has been the legacy of Hiroshima and Nagasaki?

ANSWERS TO MULTIPLE-CHOICE AND TRUE-FALSE QUESTIONS

Multiple-Choice Questions

1-A, 2-C, 3-D, 4-D, 5-D, 6-B, 7-C, 8-D

True-False Questions

1-T, 2-F, 3-T, 4-T, 5-F, 6-T, 7-T, 8-T

31

THE FAIR DEAL AND CONTAINMENT

CHAPTER OBJECTIVES

After you complete the reading and study of this chapter, you should be able to:

1. Analyze the problems of demobilization and conversion to peacetime production.
2. Account for Truman's troubles with Congress and assess the measure of accomplishment which he achieved.
3. Explain the policy of containment and trace its development to 1950.
4. Account for Truman's reelection in 1948.
5. Explain the strength of McCarthyism in the United States.
6. Explain the origins of the Korean War and trace its major developments.

CHAPTER OUTLINE

I. Demobilization under Truman
   A. The Truman style
      1. Truman's background and character
      2. Domestic proposals of 1945
      3. Relations with Congress
   B. Demobilization
      1. Rapid reduction of armed forces
      2. Escalation of birth rate
      3. Efforts for economic stabilization
   C. Efforts to control inflation
      1. Demands for wage increases

      2. A wave of strikes
      3. Truman's response to strikes
      4. Efforts to control prices
      5. The end of controls
   D. Significant legislative achievements
      1. Employment Act of 1946
      2. Control of atomic energy
   E. Congressional elections of 1946

II. Record of the Republican Congress
   A. Restrictions on labor
   B. Efforts for tax reduction
   C. Governmental reorganization
      1. Features of the National Security Act
      2. Changes in presidential succession
      3. The Hoover Commission

III. Development of the Cold War
   A. Creating the United Nations
      1. Background to the U.N.
      2. Scheme of its operations
      3. U.S. ratification of U.N. membership
   B. Trials for war criminals
      1. Nature of the trials
      2. Debate over the justice of the trials
   C. Differences with the Soviets
      1. Problems relating to eastern Europe
      2. Development of the peace treaties
      3. Proposals to control atomic energy
   D. Development of the containment policy
      1. Kennan's theory

2. Problems in Iran, Turkey, and
   Greece
3. The Truman Doctrine
4. Greek-Turkish Aid
5. The Marshall Plan
   a. The proposal
   b. European response
   c. Work of the ERP
6. Division of Germany
   a. Merger of Allied zones
   b. Berlin Blockade
   c. Berlin Airlift
   d. Creation of West and East
      Germany
7. Development of NATO
8. Establishment of Israel

IV. Truman's domestic politics
   A. Democratic divisions
   B. Truman's game plan
   C. Efforts for civil rights for blacks
   D. The 1948 election
      1. The Republican position
      2. Democratic battle over civil rights
      3. Creation of the Dixiecrats
      4. Wallace's Progressive party
      5. Nature of the campaign
      6. Election results
      7. Assessment of the results
   E. The fate of the Fair Deal

V. The Cold War heats up
   A. Point Four Program

B. China's fall to communism
   1. History of the movement in China
   2. Assessment of the Communist
      victory
C. Soviet atomic bomb
D. Work on the hydrogen bomb
E. NSC-68

VI. The Korean War
   A. Background to conflict
   B. Response to the invasion
   C. Military developments
      1. Rout of the U.N. forces
      2. Counterattack
      3. The decision to invade the North
      4. Entry of the Chinese Communists
   D. The dismissal of MacArthur
      1. Reasons for the action
      2. Reactions to the firing
   E. Negotiations for peace

VII. Another red scare
   A. Evidences of espionage
   B. The Truman loyalty program
   C. The Alger Hiss case
   D. Conviction of spies
   E. McCarthy's witch-hunt
      1. The emergence of Senator
         McCarthy
      2. Assessment of his tactics
   F. The McCarran Internal Security Act

VIII. Peace with Japan

KEY ITEMS OF CHRONOLOGY

Employment Act	1946
Truman Doctrine	1947
Greek-Turkish Aid Program	1947
Marshall Plan launched	1947
Berlin Blockade and Berlin Airlift	June 1948–May 1949
Creation of Israel	1948
Establishment of NATO	April 1949
China became Communist	1949
Sen. Joe McCarthy's speech in Wheeling, W.Va. citing Communists in the State Department	February 1950
Korean War	June 1950–July 1953
MacArthur dismissed	April, 1951

TERMS TO MASTER

Listed below are some important terms or people with which you should be familiar after you complete the study of this chapter. Explain the significance of each name or term.

1. Employment Act of 1946
2. Atomic Energy Commission
3. Henry C. Wallace
4. Taft-Hartley Act
5. National Security Act, 1947
6. Twenty-second Amendment
7. United Nations
8. Nuremberg Trials
9. George F. Kennan
10. Truman Doctrine
11. Marshall Plan
12. Berlin Blockade
13. NATO
14. Dixiecrats
15. Cold War
16. Douglas MacArthur
17. Joseph R. McCarthy

VOCABULARY BUILDING

Listed below are some words or phrases used in this chapter. Look up each word in your dictionary unless the meaning is given here.

1. tribunal
2. *ex post facto*
3. *modus vivendi*
4. inadvertent
5. veto

EXERCISES FOR UNDERSTANDING

When you have completed the reading of the chapter, answer each of the following questions. If you have difficulty, go back and reread the section of the chapter related to the question.

Multiple-Choice Questions

Select the letter of the response which best completes the statement.

1. In personality and character Truman resembled
   A. Franklin D. Roosevelt
   B. Ulysses S. Grant
   C. Woodrow Wilson
   D. Andrew Jackson

2. Truman's plan to deal with the economy after World War II was to
   A. remove all controls on the economy immediately after the war
   B. create a public works program to provide jobs for returning servicemen
   C. retain controls on rents but no other items
   D. keep price controls for at least a year after the war ended

3. The Twenty-Second Amendment
   A. limited presidents to two terms
   B. changed the presidential succession plan to make the Speaker of the House next in line after the vice-president
   C. gave to vote to 18-year-olds
   D. ended the poll-tax requirement for all federal elections

4. Trials of war criminals after World War II were criticized because they were
   A. presided over by Americans
   B. trying people for actions which were not crimes when perpetrated
   C. a violation of the Geneva Convention and the Hague Declarations
   D. held in secret

5. The Marshall Plan was designed to
   A. help European nations rebuild their armies
   B. subvert Communist nations into the capitalist camp
   C. lend money to European nations
   D. help all European nations, including Communist ones, to rebuild their wartorn economies

6. The new state of Israel was created in 1948 by
   A. formal action of the U.N. General Assembly
   B. U.S. invasion of Arab lands

C. Jewish leaders' declaration of independence in Palestine
D. the British, who had promised a homeland for the Jews
7. Strom Thurmond's effect on Truman's 1948 reelection was
A. limited to the South
B. that he took votes from Truman in the North and South
C. that he helped Truman win black votes
D. that he won no electoral votes and had little effect on the popular vote
8. The nation was ready for Joe McCarthy because of *all but which one* of the following reasons?
A. the fall of China to communism
B. the disclosure that several Russian spies were operating in Western countries
C. the Russian development of the atomic bomb
D. the failure of the Berlin Airlift

True-False Questions

Indicate whether each statement is true or false.

1. The Employment Act of 1946 provided that the federal government must establish a WPA-type jobs program whenever unemployment reached a certain level.
2. George F. Kennan was the architect of the Truman program of containment.
3. The Taft-Hartley Act outlawed unions at any plant which paid at least the minimum wage.

4. Truman gained the greatest support from the Eightieth Congress for legislation relating to foreign policy.
5. After World War II the early disagreements between the U.S. and the USSR especially centered on eastern Europe.
6. The Western occupation zones of Germany were reunited during the Berlin airlift.
7. The Soviet Union supported the U.N. assistance of South Korea because they agreed that North Korean had no right to invade the South.
8. The entry of Chinese Communists into the Korean War came after the U.N. forces were about to take over all of North Korea.

Essay Questions

1. What were the economic problems associated with conversion from war to peace and how were they handled?
2. Account for the onset of the Cold War.
3. What was the basis for the policy of containment and how was the policy implemented in the Truman era?
4. Why was Harry Truman reelected in 1948?
5. Explain the origins of the Korean War.
6. Why did Truman fire MacArthur? Was his action justified? What reactions did it bring?
7. What was the basis for Joe McCarthy's appeal to the American people? Assess the importance of his anti-Communist crusade.

READINGS

Reading 1. Arthur Schlesinger Explains the Origins of the Cold War

The origin of the Cold War is one of the more complex and controversial historiographical problems current today. The issues involve which side was responsible for the hostility that developed after World War II between the United

States and the Soviet Union. In the article excerpted here, Arthur M. Schlesinger, Jr., a prominent historian and adviser to President Kennedy, takes a position somewhat more centrist than that of the revisionists who place the blame for the Cold War on the

United States. Writing in 1967 just after he
had broken with the Johnson administration
over the Vietnam War, Schlesinger here

attempts to show just how complex the
development of the Cold War was.

The orthodox American view, as originally set forth by the American government and as reaffirmed until recently by most American
scholars, has been that the Cold War was the brave and essential
response of free men to communist aggression. Some have gone
back well before the Second World War to lay open the sources of
Russian expansionism. Geopoliticians traced the Cold War to imperial Russian strategic ambitions which in the nineteenth century led
to the Crimean War, to Russian penetration of the Balkans and the
Middle East and to Russian pressure on Britain's "lifeline" to India.
Ideologists traced it to the Communist Manifesto of 1848 ("the
violent overthrow of the bourgeoisie lays the foundation for the
sway of the proletariat"). Thoughtful observers (a phrase meant to
exclude those who speak in Dullese about the unlimited evil of
godless, atheistic, militant communism) concluded that classical
Russian imperialism and Pan-Slavism, compounded after 1917 by
Leninist messianism, confronted the West at the end of the Second
World War with an inexorable drive for domination.

The revisionist thesis is very different. In its extreme form, it is
that, after the death of Franklin Roosevelt and the end of the Second World War, the United States deliberately abandoned the wartime policy of collaboration and, exhilarated by the possession of the
atomic bomb, undertook a course of aggression of its own designed
to expel all Russian influence from Eastern Europe and to establish
democratic-capitalist states on the very border of the Soviet Union.
As the revisionists see it, this radically new American policy—or
rather this resumption by Truman of the pre-Roosevelt policy of
insensate anti-communism—left Moscow no alternative but to take
measures in defense of its own borders. The result was the Cold
War. . . .

. . . Any honest reappraisal of the origins of the Cold War requires
the imaginative leap—which should in any case be as instinctive for
the historian as it is prudent for the statesman—into the adversary's
viewpoint. We must strive to see how, given Soviet perspectives,
the Russians might conceivably have misread our signals, as we
must reconsider how intelligently we read theirs.

Nor can the historian forget the conditions under which decisions
are made, especially in a time like the Second World War. These
were tired, overworked, aging men: in 1945, Churchill was 71 years
old, Stalin had governed his country for 17 exacting years, Roosevelt
his for 12 years nearly as exacting. . . . All—even Stalin, behind his
screen of ideology—had become addicts of improvisation, relying
on authority and vituosity to conceal the fact that they were con-
stantly surprised by developments. . . . None showed great tactical
consistency, or cared much about it; all employed a certain ambigu-
ity to preserve their power to decide big issues; and it is hard to
know how to interpret anything any one of them said on any specific
occasion. . . .

Peacemaking after the Second World War was not so much a tapestry as it was a hopelessly raveled and knotted mess of yarn. Yet, for purposes of clarity, it is essential to follow certain threads. One theme indispensable to an understanding of the Cold War is the contrast between two clashing views of world order: the "universalist" view, by which all nations shared a common interest in all the affairs of the world, and the "sphere-of-influence" view, by which each great power would be assured by the other great powers of an acknowledged predominance in its own area of special interest. The universalist view assumed that national security would be guaranteed by an international organization. The sphere-of-interest view assumed that national security would be guaranteed by the balance of power. While in practice these views have by no means been incompatible (indeed, our shaky peace has been based on a combination of the two), in the abstract they involved sharp contradictions.

The tradition of American thought in these matters was universalist. . . .

The Kremlin, on the other hand, thought *only* of spheres of interest; above all, the Russians were determined to protect their frontiers, and especially their border to the west, crossed so often and so bloodily in the dark course of their history. . . .

It is now pertinent to inquire why the United States rejected the idea of stabilizing the world by division into spheres of influence and insisted on an East European strategy. . . .

The first reason is that they regarded this solution as containing within itself the seeds of a third world war. The balance-of-power idea seemed inherently unstable. . . .

. . . the second objection: that the sphere-of-inflence approach would, in the words of the State Department in 1945, "militate against the establishment and effective functioning of a broader system of general security in which all countries will have their part." The United Nations, in short, was seen as the alternative to the balance of power. . . .

Third, the universalists feared that the sphere-of-interest approach would be what Hull termed "a haven for the isolationists," who would advocate America's participation in Western Hemisphere affairs on condition that it did not participate in European or Asian affairs. . . .

Fourth, the sphere-of-interest solution meant the betrayal of the principles for which the Second World War was being fought—the Atlantic Charter, the Four Freedoms, the Declaration of the United Nations. . . .

Fifth, the sphere-of-influence solution would create difficult domestic problems in American politics. Roosevelt was aware of the six million or more Polish votes in the 1944 election. . . .

Sixth, if the Russians were allowed to overrun Eastern Europe without argument, would that satisfy them? . . .

But the great omission of the revisionists—and also the fundamental explanation of the speed with which the Cold War escalated—lies precisely in the fact that the Soviet Union was not a traditional national state. The Soviet Union was a phenomenon very different from America or Britain: it was a totalitarian state, endowed with an all-explanatory, all-consuming ideology, committed to the infallibility of government and party, still in a somewhat messianic mood, equating dissent with treason, and ruled by a dictator who, for all his quite extraordinary abilities, had his paranoid moments.

Marxism-Leninism gave the Russian leaders a view of the world according to which all societies were inexorably destined to proceed along appointed roads by appointed stages until they achieved the classless nirvana. . . .

A revisionist fallacy has been to treat Stalin as just another Realpolitik statesman, as Second World War revisionists see Hitler as just another Stresemann or Bismarck. But the record makes it clear that in the end nothing could satisfy Stalin's paranoia. His own associates failed. Why does anyone suppose that any conceivable American policy would have succeeded?

The difference between America and Russia in 1945 was that some Americans fundamentally believed that, over a long run, a modus vivendi with Russia was possible; while the Russians, so far as one can tell, believed in no more than a short-run modus vivendi with the United States.

In retrospect, if it is impossible to see the Cold War as a case of American aggression and Russian response, it is also hard to see it as a pure case of Russian aggression and American response. . . .

The Cold War could have been avoided only if the Soviet Union had not been possessed by convictions both of the infallibility of the communist word and of the inevitability of a communist world. These convictions turned an impasse between national states into a religious war, a tragedy of ability into one of necessity. One might wish that America had preserved the poise and proportion of the first years of the Cold War and had not succumbed to its own forms of self-righteousness. But the most rational American policies could hardly have averted the Cold War. Only if Russia began to recede from its messianic mission and to accept, in fact if not yet in principle, the permanence of the world of diversity, only then did the hope flicker that this long, dreary, costly contest may at last be taking forms less dramatic, less obsessive and less dangerous to the future kind.

[Arthur Schlesinger, Jr., "Origins of the Cold War," *Foreign Affairs* 46 (October 1967); 22–52]

Reading 2. Barton Bernstein Presents a Revisionist View

Barton Bernstein has been one of the leading revisionists in the controversy over the origins of the Cold War. The excerpt below will introduce the reader to the essentials of that view.

Despite some dissents, most American scholars have reached a general concensus on the origins of the Cold War. As confirmed internationalists who believe that Russia constituted a threat to America and its European allies after World War II, they have endorsed their nation's acceptance of its obligations as a world power in the forties and its desire to establish a world order of peace and prosperity. Convinced that only American efforts prevented the Soviet Union from expanding past Eastern Europe, they have generally praised the containment policies of the Truman Doctrine, the Marshall Plan, and NATO as evidence of America's acceptance of world responsibility. While chiding or condemning those on the right who opposed international involvement (or had even urged preventive war), they have also been deeply critical of those on the left who have believed that the Cold War could have been avoided, or that the United States shared substantial responsibility for the Cold War.

Despite the widespread acceptance of this interpretation, there has long been substantial evidence (and more recently a body of scholarship) which suggests that American policy was neither so innocent nor so nonideological; that American leaders sought to promote their conceptions of national interest and their values even at the conscious risk of provoking Russia's fears about her security. In 1945 these leaders aparently believed that American power would be adequate for the task of reshaping much of the world according to America's needs and standards.

By overextending policy and power and refusing to accept Soviet interests, American policy-makers contributed to the Cold War. There was little understanding of any need to restrain American political efforts and desires. Though it cannot be proved that the United States could have achieved a *modus vivendi* with the Soviet Union in these years there is evidence that Russian policies were reasonably cautious and conservative, and that there was at least a basis for accommodation. But this possibility slowly slipped away as President Harry S. Truman reversed Roosevelt's tactics of accommodation. As American demands for democratic governments in Eastern Europe became more vigorous, as the new administration delayed in providing economic assistance to Russia and in seeking international control of atomic energy, policy-makers met with increasing Soviet suspicion and antagonism. Concluding that Soviet-American cooperation was impossible, they came to believe that the Soviet state could be halted only by force or the threat of force. . . .

. . . It is clear that Truman was either incapable or unwilling to reexamine his earlier assumption (or decision) of using the bomb. Under the tutelage of Byrnes and Stimson, Truman had come to assume by July that the bomb should be used, and perhaps he was incapable of reconsidering this strategy because he found no compelling reason not to use the bomb. Or he may have consciously rejected the options because he wanted to use the bomb. Perhaps he was vindictive and wished to retaliate for Pearl Harbor and other atrocities. (In justifying the use of the bomb against the Japanese, he wrote a few days after Nagasaki, "The only language they seem to understand is the one we have been using to bombard them. When you have to deal with a beast you have to treat him as a beast.") Or, most likely, Truman agreed with Byrnes that using the bomb would advance other American policies: It would end the war before the Russians could gain a hold in Manchuria, it would permit

the United States to exclude Russia from the occupation government of Japan, and it would make the Soviets more manageable in
Eastern Europe. It would enable the United States to shape the
peace according to its own standards.

At minimum, then, the use of the bomb reveals the moral insen-
sitivity of the President—whether he used it because the moral
implications did not compel a reexamination of assumptions, or
because he sought retribution, or because he sought to keep Russia
out of Manchuria and the occupation government of Japan, and to
make her more manageable in Eastern Europe. In 1945 American
foreign policy was not innocent, nor was it unconcerned about
Russian power, nor did it assume that the United States lacked the
power to impose its will on the Russian state, nor was it characterized by high moral purpose or consistent dedication to humanitar-
ian principles.

While the Soviet Union would not generally permit in Eastern
Europe conditions that conformed to Western ideals, Stalin was
pursuing a cautious policy and seeking accommodation with the
West. He was willing to allow capitalism but was suspicious of
American efforts at economic penetration which could lead to political dominance. Though by the autumn of 1945 the governments
in Russia's general area of influence were subservient in foreign
policy, they varied in form and in degree of independence—democracy in Czechoslovakia (the only country in this area with a democratic tradition), free elections and the overthrow of the Communist
party in Hungary, a Communist-formed coalition government in
Bulgaria, a broadly based but Communist-dominated government
in Poland, and a Soviet-imposed government in Rumania (the most
anti-Russian of these nations). In all of these countries Communists
controlled the ministries of interior (the police) and were able to
suppress anti-Soviet groups, including anti-communist democrats.

Those who have attributed to Russia a policy of inexorable expansion have often neglected this immediate postwar period, or they
have interpreted it simply as a necessary preliminary (a cunning
strategy to allay American suspicions until the American Army
demobilized and left the continent) to the consolidation and extension of power in east-central Europe. From this perspective, however, much of Stalin's behavior becomes strangely contradictory
and potentially self-defeating. If he had planned to create puppets
rather than an area of "friendly governments," why (as Isaac
Deutscher asks) did Stalin "so stubbornly refuse to make any concessions to the Poles over their eastern frontiers"? Certainly, also, his
demand for reparations from Hungary, Rumania, and Bulgaria
would have been unnecessary if he had planned to take over these
countries. (America's insistence upon using a loan to Russia to
achieve political goals, and nearly twenty-month delay after Russia
first submitted a specific proposal for assistance, led Harriman to
suggest in November that the loan policy "may have contributed to
their [Russian] avaricious policies in the countries occupied or liber-
ated by the Red Army.")

Russian sources are closed, so it is not possible to prove that Soviet
intentions were conservative; nor for the same reason is it possible

for those who adherred to the thesis of inexorable Soviet expansion to prove their theory. But the available evidence better supports the thesis that these years should be viewed not as a cunning preliminary to the harshness of 1947 and afterward, but as an attempt to establish a *modus vivendi* with the West and to protect "socialism in one country." This interpretation explains more adequately why the Russians delayed nearly three years before ending dissent and hardening policies in the countries behind their own military lines. It would also explain why the Communist parties in France and Italy were cooperating with the coalition governments until these parties were forced out of the coalitions in 1947. . . .

If the Russian policy was conservative and sought accommodation (as now seems likely), then its failure must be explained by looking beyond Russian actions. Historians must reexamine this period and reconsider American policies. Were they directed toward compromise? Can they be judged as having sought adjustment? Or did they demand acquiescence to the American world view, thus thwarting real negotiations?

There is considerable evidence that American actions clearly changed after Roosevelt's death. Slowly abandoning the tactics of accommodation, they became even more vigorous after Hiroshima. The insistence upon rolling back Soviet influence in Eastern Europe, the reluctance to grant a loan for Russian reconstruction, the inability to reach an agreement on Germany, the maintenance of the nuclear monopoly—all of these could have contributed to the sense of Russian insecurity. The point, then, is that in 1945 and 1946 there may still have been possibilities for negotiations and settlements, for accommodations and adjustments, if the United States had been willing to recognize Soviet fears, to accept Soviet power in her areas of influence, and to ease anxieties.

[Barton J. Bernstein, "American Foreign Policy and the Origins of the Cold War," in *Politics and Policies of the Truman Administration*, edited by Barton J. Bernstein (Chicago: Quadrangle Books, 1970), pp. 15–49]

Questions for Reflection

After reading both excerpts and answering the questions below, attempt to write in a few paragraphs your own view of the origins of the Cold War.

What is the orthodox view of the origins of the Cold War? The revisionist view? What special considerations should be taken into account in attempting to explain the Cold War? What important theme does Schlesinger want the reader to consider in explaining the development of Cold War events? What does he think the revisionists have omitted in their analysis of the Cold War?

How does Bernstein's initial description of the consensus view of Cold War origins compare with Schlesinger's view above? Needless use of the atomic bomb is one of the central themes of revisionist history. How does Bernstein deal with this matter? How does he argue that the United States acted incorrectly in eastern Europe? How do we know Russia's motives after World War II? What limitation does that place on historians?

ANSWERS TO MULTIPLE-CHOICE
AND TRUE-FALSE QUESTIONS

Multiple-Choice Questions

1-D, 2-C, 3-A, 4-B, 5-D, 6-C, 7-C, 8-D

True-False Questions

1-F, 2-T, 3-F, 4-T, 5-T, 6-T, 7-F, 8-T

32

CONFLICT AND DEADLOCK: THE 1950s

CHAPTER OBJECTIVES

After you complete the reading and study of this chapter, you should be able to:

1. Describe the Eisenhower style and his approach to the nation's problems.
2. Assess the nature of modern Republicanism in relation to New Deal liberalism, focusing especially on Eisenhower's stance on key domestic legislation.
3. Assess the early performance of Dulles's diplomacy, especially as compared to the policy of containment.
4. Explain the origins of the Indochina War and assess Eisenhower's response to it.
5. Describe the developments in civil rights in the Eisenhower era and assess his responses to them.
6. Explain the Suez Crisis and the Hungarian Revolt, their interrelations and their consequences.
7. Assess the impact of Sputnik.

CHAPTER OUTLINE

I. The election of 1952
   A. Liabilities of the Truman administration
   B. The Republicans' choice
      1. Taft's position
      2. Eisenhower's appeal
   C. The Democratic draft
      1. The Kefauver candidacy
      2. Stevenson's nomination
   D. Nature of the campaign
   E. Results

II. Eisenhower's early leadership in domestic affairs
   A. Eisenhower's background and style
      1. Earlier career
      2. Preference for staff administrative organization
      3. Impact of the style
      4. More recent assessment of his actions
   B. The Eisenhower appointments
   C. Assessment of his conservative direction
   D. Efforts to repeal Democratic policies
      1. Tidelands to the states
      2. Abolition of Reconstruction Finance Corporation
      3. The move away from public power
      4. Cutting the budget
   E. Extension of New Deal programs
      1. Social Security benefits
      2. Minimum-wage increases
      3. Low-income housing
      4. Farm programs
         a. REA and farm loans
         b. Surplus farm products

F. Major public works programs
   1. St. Lawrence Seaway
   2. Interstate Highway System
G. Concluding an armistice in Korea
   1. Means of obtaining agreement
   2. Terms of the armistice
   3. Factors influencing the change
H. Concluding the McCarthy witch-hunt
   1. McCarthy clashes with the new
      administration
   2. McCarthy's battle with the army
   3. The dénouement of McCarthy
I. New efforts for internal security
J. The Warren Court

III. Foreign policy
   A. The background of John Foster
      Dulles
   B. A policy of "liberation"
      1. Relationship to containment
         policies
      2. Liberation betrayed
   C. Convert actions
      1. Iran
      2. Guatemala
   D. Policy of "massive retaliation"
   E. Theory of "brinksmanship"
   F. The problems of Indochina
      1. Ending colonialism in Southeast
         Asia
         a. Independence of British colonies
         b. Creation of independent
            Indonesia
         c. Ho Chi Minh's efforts for
            independence in Indochina
      2. First Indochinese War
         a. Onset of the war
         b. Increasing American aid
         c. Eisenhower's domino theory
      3. The Geneva Accords
         a. French defeats
         b. Provisions of the accords
         c. Reactions
   G. Creation of SEATO
   H. Vietnamese government under Diem
      1. Need for reform
      2. Diem's effort to maintain power
      3. Emergence of the NLF
   I. The issue of Quemoy and Matsu
   J. A thaw in the Cold War
      1. Austrian treaty
      2. Geneva Summit Conference

IV. The affluent society

A. The consumer economy
   1. Nature of economic prosperity
   2. New products
   3. Relaxed trade restrictions
   4. Statistical evidence of growth
B. Stirrings in civil rights
   1. Eisenhower's stance on civil rights
   2. Court decisions
      a. Decisions preliminary to *Brown*
      b. The *Brown* decision
      c. Reactions to *Brown*
         i. Eisenhower's reluctance
         ii. Token integration
         iii. Massive resistance
   3. The Montgomery bus boycott
      a. Cause for action
      b. Role of Martin Luther King, Jr.
      c. Results
   4. Civil rights legislation
   5. Little Rock
   6. The collapse of massive resistance
      in Virginia
C. The election of 1956
   1. Ike's health
   2. The Democratic campaign
   3. Results

V. A season of troubles
   A. The Suez crisis
      1. Eisenhower's Middle East policy
      2. The courting of Nasser
      3. Cancellation of the loan offer
      4. Nasser's seizure of Suez
      5. The Israeli invasion
      6. Resolution of the issues
   B. The Hungarian revolt
   C. The budget battle of 1957
   D. The impact of Sputnik
      1. The Russian feat
      2. American reactions
         a. The American space effort
         b. Deployment of missiles
         c. Creation of NASA
         d. National Defense Education Act
   E. Signs of corruption in the
      administration
   F. Democratic congressional gains
   G. Final legislative gains
      1. Landrum-Griffin Act
      2. Statehood for Alaska and Hawaii

VI. Other problems abroad
   A. The Eisenhower Doctrine
   B. Lebanese intervention

C. Quemoy and Matsu again
D. The Berlin problem
E. The U-2 Summit
   1. The spy plane downed
   2. Eisenhower's fumbling reaction
   3. Khrushchev's response
F. Japanese troubles

G. Castro's Cuba
   1. Castro's takeover
   2. American responses
VII. Assessing the Eisenhower years
   A. Accomplishments
   B. The Farewell Address

KEY ITEMS OF CHRONOLOGY

Fall of Dien Bien Phu	May 1954
Brown v. Board of Education	May 1954
Geneva Accords signed	July 1954
SEATO created	September 1954
McCarthy condemned by the Senate	December 1954
Montgomery Bus boycott	December 1955–December 1956
Suez Crisis (and Hungarian Revolt)	October 1956
Little Rock High School crisis	September 1957
Sputnik launched	October 1957
U-2 Incident	May 1960

TERMS TO MASTER

Listed below are some important terms or people with which you should be familiar after you complete the study of this chapter. Explain the significance of each name or term.

1. Adlai Stevenson
2. "dynamic conservatism"
3. St. Lawrence Seaway
4. Interstate Highway System
5. Earl Warren
6. "liberation"
7. "massive retaliation"
8. Ho Chi Minh
9. Dien Bien Phu
10. Geneva Accords
11. SEATO
12. Quemoy and Matsu
13. *Brown v. Board of Education*
14. Martin Luther King, Jr.
15. Suez Crisis
16. Sputnik
17. U-2 Incident

VOCABULARY BUILDING

Listed below are some words or phrases used in this chapter. Look up each word in your dictionary unless the meaning is given here.

1. dissimulation
2. syntax
3. innuendo
4. lexicon

EXERCISES FOR UNDERSTANDING

When you have completed the reading of the chapter, answer each of the following questions. If you have difficulty, go back and reread the section of the chapter related to the question.

Multiple-Choice Questions

Select the letter of the response which best completes the statement.

1. The Eisenhower administration promised and sought to make a break with the previous Democratic administrations in
   A. domestic policy only
   B. foreign policy only
   C. both domestic and foreign policy
   D. neither domestic nor foreign policy

2. Eisenhower's presidency differed from previous administrations in his tendency to
   A. push issues more vigorously with Congress
   B. be more actively involved in foreign policy than his predecessors
   C. rely on a staff system to protect him from too much information and work
   D. be more interested in cultural and intellectual pursuits

3. Which of the following was a way in which Eisenhower sought to undo New Deal policies?
   A. abolition of the RFC
   B. encouragement of private power
   C. returning control of undersea oil lands to the states
   D. all of the above

4. The main stumbling block to a Korean peace was
   A. the death of Joseph Stalin
   B. the Communist insistence on our returning even those prisoners who did not want to go back home
   C. Eisenhower's threat to use nuclear weapons to end the war
   D. MacArthur's desire for total victory in the war

5. Senator McCarthy met his downfall as a result of a direct conflict with
   A. Eisenhower, whom he called a Communist
   B. the FBI
   C. the State Department
   D. The United States Army

6. Massive retaliation as a defense measure was designed to
   A. give the military more flexibility to respond to different kinds of world crises
   B. provide an appropriate response to the Hungarian revolt
   C. make equivalent countermoves to Soviet power

D. save defense funds for the United States

7. An important criticism of the Eisenhower administration in relation to the Geneva Accords would be
   A. the United States was not present when the Accords were developed
   B. the U.S. gave no aid to Vietnam after 1954
   C. Diem brought significant reform to South Vietnam under our direction
   D. the United States did not insist on an election in 1956 as provided in the Accords

8. Eisenhower's Farewell Address dealt with
   A. the need for greater military spending
   B. the dangers of a military-industrial complex
   C. how to solve problems of civil rights
   D. the need for a better highway system

True-False Questions

Indicate whether each statement is true or false.

1. During the Eisenhower administration no effort was made to extend Social Security benefits.

2. The Eisenhower administration was especially strong in its denunciation of U.S. policy commitments made at Yalta.

3. Both the British and the Dutch gave up colonies in Southeast Asia before the French did.

4. An important issue in the campaign of 1956 was Eisenhower's health.

5. The Eisenhower administration opposed all forms of massive federal public works programs.

6. Eisenhower refused to make positive statements to support the Supreme Court's *Brown* decision.

7. The Suez Crisis involved the U.S. support for, then refusal to support, the Aswan Dam project in Egypt.

8. The NDEA was a United States response to the launching of Sputnik.

Essay Questions

1. How did Ike's administrative style and philosophy differ from those characterizing the New Deal? How successful was he in repealing Democratic programs?
2. What factors contributed to the fall of Senator McCarthy?
3. How did the Dulles foreign policy differ from containment? Was the Dulles policy genuinely different or did it simply give the illusion of being different? Explain.
4. Assess America's involvement in Vietnam during the Eisenhower administration.
5. Trace the major developments in civil rights during the 1950s. What was Eisenhower's attitude and reaction?
6. Account for the United States position in both the Suez Crisis and the Hungarian Revolts of 1956.
7. Explain the U.S. reaction to the launching of Sputnik.

DOCUMENT

Demographic Statistics of the Postwar Era

The following charts display a number of population trends of the postwar era, and especially of the 1950s. The information presented here will help you to understand better the social history of the 1950s. [The charts are adapted from materials in United States Bureau of the Census, *Historical Statistics of the United States* (Washington, D.C.: U.S. Government Printing Office, 1976), pp. 8, 49, 64, 96, 391, 401.]

Chart 1. Population, Marriages, Divorces, Birth Rate, Religion, and Farm Population, 1940–1970

In this chart, all figures (except birth rates) are in thousands, which means that you should add 000 to the numbers shown. Thus a population in 1960 of 180,671 is actually 180,671,000. Birth rates are per 1000 people in the total population. "Religion" refers to the membership of all religious groups.

Year	Total Population	No. Marriages	No. Divorces	Birth Rate	Religion	Farm Population
1970	204,879	2,163	708	18.4	131,046	9,712
1969	202,677	2,145	639	17.8	128,505	10,307
1968	200,706	2,069	584	17.5	128,470	10,454
1967	198,712	1,927	523	17.8	126,445	10,875
1966	196,560	1,857	499	18.4	123,826	11,595
1965	194,303	1,800	479	19.4	124,682	12,363
1964	191,889	1,725	450	21.0	123,307	12,954
1963	189,242	1,654	428	21.7	120,965	13,367
1962	186,538	1,577	413	22.4	117,946	14,313
1961	183,691	1,548	414	23.3	116,110	14,803
1960	180,671	1,523[a]	393[a]	23.7[a]	114,449	15,635[a]
1959	177,830[a]	1,494[b]	395[b]	24.0[b]	112,227[a]	16,592[b]
1958	174,141	1,451	368	24.5	109,558[b]	17,128

Year	Total Population	No. Marriages	No. Divorces	Birth Rate	Religion	Farm Population
1957	171,274	1,518	381	25.3	104,190	17,656
1956	168,221	1,585	382	25.2	103,225	18,712
1955	165,275	1,531	377	25.0	100,163	19,078
1954	162,391	1,490	379	25.3	97,483	19,019
1953	159,565	1,546	390	25.0	94,843	19,874
1952	156,954	1,539	392	25.1	92,277	21,748
1951	154,287	1,595	381	24.9	88,673	21,890
1950	151,684	1,667	385	24.1	86,830	23,048
1949	149,188	1,580	397	24.5	81,862	24,194
1948	146,631	1,811	408	24.9	79,436	24,383
1947	144,126	1,992	483	26.6	77,386	25,829
1946	141,389	2,291	610	24.1	73,673	25,403
1945	139,928	1,613	485	20.4	71,700	24,420
1944	138,397	1,452	400	21.2	72,493	24,815
1943	136,739	1,577	359	22.7	n/a	26,186
1942	134,860	1,772	321	22.2	68,501	28,914
1941	133,402	1,696	293	20.3	n/a	30,118
1940	132,122	1,596	264	19.4	64,502	30,547

[a] Year in which both Alaska and Hawaii were included in the figures.
[b] Year in which Alaska was included in the figures.

Chart 2. Recreational Pursuits

This chart shows comparative figures for some recreational pursuits of Americans between 1940 and 1970. "Total $" refers to the total dollar amount (in thousands of dollars) spent for a variety of recreational supplies and pursuits, including toys, sports equipment, boats, bicycles, radio and television receivers and repair, clubs and fraternal organizations, parimutuel tracks, books and maps, magazines, flowers and potted plants, and other miscellaneous goods and activities. "Radio-TV" refers to the dollar amount (in thousands of dollars) spent to purchase radio and television receivers. "Books" refers to the dollar amount (in thousands of dollars) spent to purchase books and maps. "Attendance" refers to the total attendance (in thousands) at movie theaters, spectator sports, and other kinds of theater entertainment. "Movies" refers to the number of persons (in thousands) attending movie theaters. "Sports" refers to the number of persons (in thousands) attending spectator-sports events.

All figures beginning with 1960 include Alaska and Hawaii.

Year	Total $	Radio-TV ($)	Books ($)	Magazines ($)	Attendance	Movies	Sports
1970	39,049	8,328	3,441	4,097	2,413	1,162	516
1969	36,284	7,838	3,172	3,798	2,260	1,099	487
1968	33,623	7,715	2,825	3,508	2,130	1,045	453
1967	30,758	7,328	2,689	3,207	2,030	989	436
1966	28,850	6,905	2,365	3,059	1,923	964	414
1965	26,298	6,013	2,061	2,868	1,811	927	389
1964	24,571	5,409	1,969	2,735	1,762	913	365

Year	Total $	Radio-TV ($)	Books ($)	Magazines ($)	Attendance	Movies	Sports
1963	22,213	4,539	1,620	2,521	1,692	904	342
1962	20,474	3,935	1,523	2,415	1,646	903	326
1961	19,506	3,668	1,396	2,348	1,625	921	306
1960	18,295	3,412	1,304	2,193	1,606	951	290
1959	17,381	3,330	1,159	2,110	1,571	958	269
1958	15,817	2,836	1,022	2,061	1,538	992	249
1957	15,333	2,825	983	1,973	1,655	1,126	242
1956	14,979	2,938	951	1,880	1,899	1,394	237
1955	14,078	2,869	867	1,869	1,801	1,326	230
1954	13,077	2,726	806	1,825	1,672	1,228	224
1953	12,720	2,588	830	1,776	1,605	1,187	221
1952	12,102	2,349	788	1,689	1,655	1,246	220
1951	11,564	2,236	776	1,573	1,716	1,310	220
1950	11,147	2,421	674	1,495	1,781	1,376	222
1949	10,010	1,675	627	1,454	1,872	1,451	239
1948	9,692	1,450	584	1,374	1,918	1,506	232
1947	9,249	1,398	531	1,243	2,003	1,594	222
1946	8,539	1,116	589	1,099	2,066	1,692	200
1945	6,139	344	520	965	1,714	1,450	116
1944	5,422	311	450	880	1,563	1,341	80
1943	4,961	403	366	838	1,455	1,275	62
1942	4,677	634	291	703	1,204	1,022	90
1941	4,239	607	255	636	995	809	107
1940	3,761	494	234	589	904	735	98

Chart 3. Marriage and Divorce Rates

This chart shows the rate of marriages and divorces per 1,000 total population. Figures after 1959 include Alaska and after 1960 include Hawaii.

Year	Marriage	Divorce	Year	Marriage	Divorce
1970	10.6	3.5	1950	11.1	2.6
1969	10.6	3.2	1949	10.6	2.7
1968	10.4	2.9	1948	12.4	2.8
1967	9.7	2.6	1947	13.9	3.4
1966	9.5	2.5	1946	16.4	4.3
1965	9.3	2.5	1945	12.2	3.5
1964	9.0	2.4	1944	10.9	2.9
1963	8.8	2.3	1943	11.7	2.6
1962	8.5	2.2	1942	13.2	2.4
1961	8.5	2.3	1941	12.7	2.2

Year	Marriage	Divorce	Year	Marriage	Divorce
1960	8.5	2.2	1940	12.1	2.0
1959	8.5	2.2			
1958	8.4	2.1			
1957	8.9	2.2			
1956	9.5	2.3			
1955	9.3	2.3			
1954	9.2	2.4			
1953	9.8	2.5			
1952	9.9	2.5			
1951	10.4	2.5			

Questions for Reflection

Interpreting statistics like those shown above is often necessary in historical work and in everyday life. Statistical interpretation often requires noting percentage increases and decreases, assessing relative rates of particular activities, and simply examining figures for long-term trends. The questions below will require that you make some of these comparisons.

(To obtain the rate of increase or decrease in trends like these, you simply subtract the figure for one year from that of another and then divide the difference by the figure for the year of reference. Thus if you want to know the rate of population increase from 1955 to 1956, you subtract 165,275 from 168,221 to get 2,946. Then divide that by 165,275 to see that the population increased by 1.8% from 1955 to 1956.)

What trends do the statistics show about farm population in the United States during these years?

What trend is evident in the rate of births from World War II through the 1950s? What is the implication of this trend? How can you explain the trend in birth rates during the 1960s as compared with the 1950s?

What is the trend evident in the changing rates of marriage and divorce during these years?

In what year was the divorce rate highest?

How can you explain that? What happened to the marriage rate during and after World War II?

In what year did the expenditures for radio and television sets show a dramatic increase? How do you account for that increase?

When did movie attendance begin to decline? Can you account for that decline? When did attendance increase again? What percentage of the total population attended movies in 1950, 1956, 1970? (Use Charts 1 and 2 to answer this question.)

Did the growth of television seem to cause a decline in the purchase of books and magazines? (When considering increases in dollar figures for something like the purchase of books, does a small increase in the dollar amount spent from year to year necessarily indicate an increase in the number of books purchased? What would be the effect of inflation or price increases upon these figures? What other information would you need to know in order to assess the impact of inflation on consumer behavior as indicated on this chart?)

What other trends do you see as you examine these figures carefully, focusing primarily upon the decade of the 1950s but using the forties and sixties for comparison?

ANSWERS TO MULTIPLE-CHOICE
AND TRUE-FALSE QUESTIONS

Multiple-Choice Questions

1-C, 2-C, 3-D, 4-B, 5-D, 6-D, 7-D, 8-B

True-False Questions

1-F, 2-F, 3-T, 4-T, 5-F, 6-T, 7-T, 8-T

33

INTO THE MAELSTROM: THE SIXTIES

CHAPTER OBJECTIVES

After you complete the reading and study of this chapter, you should be able to:

1. Describe the demographic trends of the 1950s and 1960s, and show their relationship to social and political developments.
2. Describe Kennedy's style and compare it to those of his predecessor and successor.
3. Assess Kennedy's domestic legislative achievements.
4. Assess the Kennedy record in foreign affairs.
5. Describe and account for LBJ's legislative accomplishments.
6. Explain why the Vietnam War became a quagmire for the United States and why LBJ changed his policy there in 1968.
7. Trace the transformation of the civil rights movement into the black power movement.
8. Describe the counterculture and explain its development and goals.

CHAPTER OUTLINE

I. The uncertain conclusion of the fifties
   A. Criticisms of affluence
   B. The Commission on National Goals

   C. The development of disobedience and rebellion
II. Demographic and economic trends
   A. The cult of youth
   B. The expectation of older groups
   C. Population decline and consequences
   D. An urban nation
     1. The urban majority
     2. Sunbelt growth
     3. Suburban growth
     4. Social problems of the cities
   E. Economic growth
     1. Statistical evidence
     2. Federal responsibility for growth
   F. Maldistribution of wealth
     1. The American social structure
     2. The poor
III. Kennedy's New Frontier
   A. The election of 1960
     1. Nixon and Kennedy as candidates
     2. The campaign
       a. Neutralization of religion
       b. The television debates
     3. Results
   B. Kennedy's administration
     1. Caliber of appointments
     2. Nature of the Kennedy style
   C. The domestic record
     1. Congressional conservatism
     2. The tax-cut proposal
     3. Legislative successes
       a. Foreign aid

  b. Peace Corps
  c. Trade expansion
  d. Housing assistance
  e. Increased minimum wage
  f. Area development
  g. Space race
D. Foreign frontiers
  1. Bay of Pigs disaster
  2. Vienna Summit
  3. Berlin Wall
  4. Cuban Missile Crisis
    a. Nature of the crisis
    b. Kennedy's action
    c. Resolution of the crisis
    d. Aftereffects
      i. Lowered tension
      ii. Sale of wheat
      iii. Washington-Moscow
         hotline
      iv. Removal of obsolete
         missiles
      v. Nuclear test ban treaty
  5. Neutrality for Laos
  6. Vietnam
    a. Diem's failure to reform or gain
       popular support
    b. Kennedy's reluctance to
       escalate
    c. Heightened opposition to
       Diem
    d. Overthrow of Diem
E. The Kennedy assassination

IV. Lyndon Johnson and the Great Society
  A. Johnson's background and style
  B. His mastery of politics and
     Congress
  C. Early legislative achievements
    1. The tax cut
    2. The War on Poverty
  D. The election of 1964
    1. Republicans seek a "choice"
    2. Goldwater's weaknesses
    3. Johnson's appeal to consensus
    4. The Johnson landslide
  E. Landmark legislation
    1. Health insurance
    2. Aid to education
    3. Appalachian redevelopment
    4. Housing and urban development

V. The Civil Rights Revolution: from rights
   to black power
  A. The civil rights movement since 1955
  B. The Freedom Rides

  C. The integration of "Ole Miss"
  D. Demonstrations in Birmingham
  E. The confrontation with George
     Wallace
  F. The Washington March
  G. The Civil Rights Act of 1964
  H. The Voting Rights Act of 1965
    1. The Selma March
    2. Provisions of the Voting Rights
       Act
  I. The development of black power
    1. The riots of 1965 and 1966
    2. Assessment of the urban black
       condition
    3. The focus on black power
      a. Stokely Carmichael
      b. The Black Panthers
      c. Malcolm X
      d. Assessment of black power

VI. The tragedy of Vietnam
  A. An effort to avoid defeat
    1. Escalation
    2. The cost of the war
  B. The Tonkin Gulf Resolution
    1. Basis for the request
    2. Provisions of the resolution
  C. Escalation in 1965
    1. Attack on Pleiku
    2. "Operation Rolling Thunder"
    3. Combat troops
  D. The context for policy
    1. Consistency with earlier foreign
       policy goals
    2. Warnings from advisers
    3. The goal of United States
       involvement
    4. The erosion of support
  E. The turning point of the war
    1. The Tet Offensive
    2. The presidential primaries
    3. Johnson's decision to move out

VII. The crescendo of the sixties
  A. The tragedies of 1968
    1. Martin Luther King, Jr.
    2. Robert Kennedy
  B. The counterculture
    1. Students for a Democratic Society
    2. Free Speech Movement
    3. Criticism and disruption of
       colleges
    4. The composition of the New
       Left
    5. The heritage of youth revolt

C. Convergence on the election of 1968
   1. Chicago demonstrations
   2. The contrast of Miami

3. The Wallace campaign
4. The results

KEY ITEMS OF CHRONOLOGY

Bay of Pigs invasion	April 1961
Freedom Rides	May 1961
SDS organized	1962
Cuban Missile Crisis	October 1963
Overthrow of Ngo Dinh Diem	November 1963
Kennedy assassination	November 1963
Free Speech Movement at Berkeley	1964
Civil Rights Act (public accommodations)	July 1964
Gulf of Tonkin Resolution	August 1964
Voting Rights Act	1965
Tet Offensive	January–February 1968

TERMS TO MASTER

Listed below are some important terms or people with which you should be familiar after you complete the study of this chapter. Explain the significance of each name or term.

1. "baby-boom" generation
2. "Sunbelt"
3. Peace Corps
4. Bay of Pigs invasion
5. Berlin Wall
6. Cuban Missile Crisis
7. Nuclear Test Ban Treaty
8. Ngo Dinh Diem
9. Medicare and Medicaid
10. SNCC
11. Freedom Rides
12. March on Washington
13. Watts riots
14. black power
15. Stokely Carmichael
16. Malcolm X
17. Gulf of Tonkin Resolution
18. Vietcong
19. Eugene McCarthy
20. Robert Kennedy
21. Port Huron Statement
22. counterculture
23. New Left

VOCABULARY BUILDING

Listed below are some words or phrases used in this chapter. Look up each word in your dictionary unless the meaning is given here.

1. maelstrom
2. protean
3. cornucopia
4. pundits
5. banal
6. euphemism
7. immolate

EXERCISES FOR UNDERSTANDING

When you have completed the reading of the chapter, answer each of the following questions. If you have difficulty, go back and reread the section of the chapter related to the question.

Multiple-Choice Questions

Select the letter of the response which best completes the statement.

1. Eisenhower's national goals commission concluded that

A. America needed more national direction
B. the United States had nothing to fear from communism
C. there was no need to worry about America's future
D. the United States needed to invest more in education in order to survive

2. The baby-boom generation caused
   A. a need for more schools in the 1960s
   B. a demand for more housing in the 1950s
   C. a demand for more jobs in the 1970s
   D. all of the above

3. By 1970 the largest group of Americans lived
   A. on farms
   B. in central cities
   C. in suburbs
   D. in northern cities

4. The election of 1960 resulted in
   A. Kennedy's victory by the narrowest popular vote margin since 1888
   B. Nixon's winning more states than Kennedy
   C. Kennedy's winning key southern states on the basis of black votes
   D. all of the above

5. Kennedy's most important legislative achievement was
   A. the Peace Corps
   B. the Civil Rights Act
   C. the Trade Expansion Act
   D. Medicare

6. Johnson got the tax-cut bill passed by
   A. reducing the budget below $100 billion
   B. asking voluntary tax contributions from businessmen
   C. linking the tax cut to the need for less military spending
   D. all of the above

7. The urban riots of 1965 and 1966 were started by
   A. blacks fed up with their situation
   B. whites aiming to destroy blacks
   C. the police, while chasing looters
   D. the Johnson administration, in order to get support for its urban programs

8. Johnson sought to deescalate the Vietnam War because

A. the Tet Offensive showed that we could not win
B. political challengers showed the high level of public opposition to the war
C. key national leaders called on him to end the war
D. all of the above

True-False Questions

Indicate whether each statement is true or false.

1. After he came into office, Kennedy discovered that there was no missile gap with the Soviets.
2. The Berlin Wall was primarily designed to keep spies out of East Germany.
3. Kennedy supported neutrality for Laos.
4. Goldwater opposed the nuclear test ban and the Civil Rights Act.
5. The sit-in movement began on a bus trip to Alabama.
6. The Voting Rights Act of 1965 ended literacy tests in countries and states where fewer than half the adults had voted in 1964.
7. Malcolm X was killed by a white segregationist.
8. The Gulf of Tonkin Resolution was approved by Congress on the basis of inaccurate information about attacks on the United States.

Essay Questions

1. What generalizations can you draw from the text's discussion of population trends in the 1950s and 1960s?
2. What weaknesses were apparent in the American economy of the 1960s?
3. Account for Kennedy's victory and its narrow proportions in 1960.
4. What was meant by the Great Society? Evaluate its development and effectiveness.
5. What were the major milestones in the Vietnam conflict between 1961 and 1968?
6. How effective was the civil rights movement of the 1960s?
7. What is meant by the counterculture?

Explain its composition, origins, goals,   8. Account for the election of Richard
and impact.   Nixon in 1968.

DOCUMENT

The Pentagon Papers Assess the Effectiveness of Bombing in Vietnam

The *Pentagon Papers*, a lengthy assessment
of Vietnam policy which had been
commissioned by Secretary of Defense
Robert McNamara, was released in 1971
through the efforts of Daniel Ellsburg. The
twelve-volume reports surveyed many
aspects of the history of the war in Vietnam.

The excerpts below discuss the effectiveness
of America's bombing of North Vietnam.
Operation "Rolling Thunder" was the code
name applied to bombing missions over
North Vietnam (referred to as NVN and
DRV—the People's Democratic Republic of
Vietnam).

318 ROLLING THUNDER aircraft were lost during 1966, as compared with 171 in 1965 (though the loss rate dropped from .66% of
attack sorties in 1965 to .39% in 1966). CIA estimated that the
direct operational cost of the program (i.e., production costs of aircraft lost, plus direct sortie overhead costs—not including air base
or logistical support—plus ordnance costs) came to $1,247 million
in 1966 as compared with $460 million in 1965.

Economic damage to NVN went up from $36 million in 1965 to
$94 million in 1966, and military damage from $34 million to $36
million. As CIA computed it, however, it cost the U.S. $9.6 to inflict
$1 worth of damage in 1966, as compared with $6.6 in 1965.

Estimated civilian and military casualties in NVN also went up,
from 13,000 to 23–24,000 (about 80% civilians), but the numbers
remained small relative to the 18 million population.

The program in 1966 had accomplished little more than in 1965,
however. In January 1967, an analysis by CIA concluded that the
attacks had not eliminated any important sector of the NVN economy or the military establishment. They had not succeeded in cut-
ting route capacities south of Hanoi to the point where the flow of
supplies required in SVN was significantly impeded. . . . 32% of
NVN's power-generating capacity had been put out of action, but
the remaining capacity was adequate to supply most industrial con-
sumers. Hundreds of bridges were knocked down, but virtually all
of them had been quickly repaired, replaced, or bypassed, and
traffic continued. Several thousand freight cars, trucks, barges, and
other vehicles were also destroyed or damaged, but inventories
were maintained through imports and there was no evidence of a
serious transport problem due to equipment shortages. The railroad
and highway networks were considerably expanded and improved
during the year.

The main losses to the economy, according to the CIA analysis,
had been indirect—due to a reduction in agricultural output and
the fish catch, a cut in foreign exchange earnings because of a
decline in exports, disruptions of production because of dispersal
and other passive defense measures, and the diversion of effort to
repair essential transportation facilities. On the military side, dam-

age had disrupted normal military practices, caused the abandonment of many facilities, and forced the widespread dispersal of
equipment, but overall military capabilities had continued at a high
level.

The summary CIA assessment was that ROLLING THUNDER
had not helped either to reduce the flow of supplies South or to
shake the will of the North:

The bombing had not succeeded in materially lowering morale
among the people, despite some "war weariness." The leaders continued to repeat in private as well as public that they were willing
to withstand even heavier bombing rather than accept a settlement
on less than their terms. As to the future: "There may be some
degree of escalation which would force the regime to reexamine its
position, but we believe that as far as pressure from air attack is
concerned the regime would be prepared to continue the insur-
gency indefinitely in the face of the current level and type of bombing program."

A key factor in sustaining the will of the regime, according to the
CIA analysis, was the "massive" economic and military aid provided
by the USSR, China, and Eastern Europe. . . .

Thus, as 1966 drew to a close, the lines were drawn for a long fifteen
month internal Administration struggle over whether to stop the
bombing and start negotiations. McNamara and his civilian advisers
had been disillusioned in 1966 with the results of the bombing and
held no sanguine hopes for the ability of air power, massively applied, to produce anything but the same inconclusive results at far
higher levels of overall hostility and with significant risk of Chinese
and/or Soviet intervention. The military, particularly CINCPAC
[Commander-in-Chief, Pacific], were ever more adamant that only
civilian imposed restraints on targets had prevented the bombing
from bringing the DRV to its knees and its senses about its aggression in the South. The principle remained sound, they argued; a
removal of limitations would produce dramatic results. And so, 1967
would be the year in which many of the previous restrictions were
progressively lifted and the vaunting boosters of air power would
be once again proven wrong. It would be the year in which we
relearned the negative lessons of previous wars on the ineffective-
ness of strategic bombing.

The lesson of the Tet offensive concerning the bombing should have
been unmistakably clear for its proponents and critics alike. Bombing to interdict the flow of men and supplies to the South had been
a signal failure. The resources necessary to initiate an offensive of
Tet proportions and sustain the casualties and munitions expenditures it entailed had all flowed south in spite of the heavy bombing
in North Vietnam, Laos and South Vietnam. It was now clear that
bombing alone could not prevent the communists from amassing
the matériel, and infiltrating the manpower necessary to conduct
massive operations if they chose. Moreover, Tet demonstrated that
the will to undergo the required sacrifices and hardships was more
than ample.

To be sure, the bombing had not been conducted to its fullest potential, but on the other hand it had been much heavier and had gone on much longer than many if not most of its advocates had expected at the outset. . . . What can be said in the end is that its partial suspension in part did produce what most had least expected —a breakthrough in the deadlock over negotiations. And that in the longer view of history may turn out to be its most significant contribution.

[U.S. Congress, House, Committee on Armed Services, *United States–Vietnam Relations, 1945–1967: Study Prepared by the Department of Defense*, Book 6 of 12 (Washington, D.C.: U.S. Government Printing Office, 1971), IV.C.7(a) vol. 1, *The Air War in North Vietnam*, pp. 178–80; IV.C.7. (b) vol. 2, *The Air War in North Vietnam*, pp. 144, 204]

Questions for Reflection

What was the cost to the United States of the air war conducted over the North? What was the effect of the bombing on the North Vietnamese? What was the subject of debate between military and civilian authorities in regard to the air war? What negative diplomatic and military consequence of intensified bombing is implied in the passage? How can you explain the continued bombing of Vietnam after 1968, given the report of its effects?

ANSWERS TO MULTIPLE-CHOICE AND TRUE-FALSE QUESTIONS

Multiple-Choice Questions

1-C, 2-D, 3-C, 4-D, 5-C, 6-A, 7-A, 8-D

True-False Questions

1-T, 2-F, 3-T, 4-T, 5-F, 6-T, 7-F, 8-T

34

THE 1970s AND BEYOND:
THE SEARCH FOR STABILITY

CHAPTER OBJECTIVES

After you complete the reading and study of this chapter, you should be able to:

1. Explain Nixon's aims in Vietnam.
2. Assess the impact of the Vietnam War on American society, military morale, and later foreign policy.
3. Explain Nixon's goals in domestic policy and account for his limited accomplishment.
4. Explain the problems plaguing the United States economy in the decade of the 1970s, and describe the various cures tried by Nixon, Ford, Carter, and Reagan.
5. Describe Nixon's foreign policy triumphs in China and the Soviet Union, and explain their significance.
6. Discuss the Watergate coverup and account for the difficulty in unraveling it.
7. Trace the reform movements for women, Hispanics, Indians, and the environment.
8. Describe the major thrusts of the Reagan presidency.

CHAPTER OUTLINE

I. The sixties as a state of mind
II. Nixon and Vietnam
   A. The policy of gradual withdrawal
   B. Movement on three fronts
      1. Insistance on Communist withdrawal from South Vietnam
      2. Efforts to undercut unrest in the United States
         a. Troop reductions
         b. Lottery and volunteer army
      3. Expanded air war
   C. Impact of the war on military morale
      1. Military disobedience
      2. Fraggings
      3. Drug problems
   D. Occasions for public outcry against the war
      1. My Lai massacre
      2. Cambodian "incursion"
         a. Campus riots
         b. Public reaction
      3. *Pentagon Papers*
         a. Method of disclosure
         b. Revelations of the papers
         c. Supreme Court ruling
   E. American withdrawal
      1. Kissinger's efforts before the 1972 election

2. The Christmas bombings
3. Final acceptance of peace
4. U.S. withdrawal in March 1973
  F. Ultimate victory of the North: March–April 1975
  G. Assessment of the war
    1. Communist control
    2. Failure to transfer democracy
    3. Erosion of respect for the military
    4. Drastic division of the American people
    5. Impact on future foreign policy

III. Nixon and Middle America
  A. A reflection of Middle American values
  B. Domestic affairs
    1. Status of Nixon in domestic legislation
    2. Continuance of civil rights progress
      a. Voting Rights Act continued over a veto
      b. Supreme Court upholds integration
        i. In Mississippi
        ii. Support for busing
      c. Congress refuses to end busing
      d. Limitation on busing in Detroit
      e. The *Bakke* decision
    3. The liberal precedents of the Warren Court
      a. *Engel v. Vitale* (1962)
      b. *Baker v. Carr* (1962)
      c. *Gideon v. Wainwright* (1963)
      d. *Miranda v. Arizona* (1966)
    4. Nixon's appointees
      a. Efforts for Haynsworth and Carswell
      b. The Nixon appointments
    5. The effort to fight crime
      a. Preventive detention
      b. No-knock legislation
    6. The proposal for welfare reform
      a. Nature of the Family Assistance Plan
      b. Reasons for rejection
    7. Revenue sharing
    8. Other domestic legislation
  C. The economic malaise
    1. The development of stagflation
    2. Causes
    3. Nixon's efforts to improve the economy

      a. Reducing the federal deficit
      b. Reducing the money supply
      c. Imposing wage and price controls

IV. Nixon's foreign triumphs
  A. Rapprochement with China
    1. Background to the visit
    2. Benefits of the Nixon visit
  B. Détente with the Soviet Union
    1. The visit to Moscow
    2. The SALT agreement
    3. Trade agreements
  C. Kissinger's shuttle diplomacy in the Middle East

V. The election of 1972
  A. Removal of the Wallace threat
  B. The McGovern candidacy
  C. Results of the election

VI. Watergate
  A. Judge Sirica's role
  B. Unraveling the coverup
    1. Nixon's personal role
    2. The development of illegal tactics
    3. April resignations
    4. Discovery of the tapes
    5. The Saturday Night Massacre
    6. The Court decides against the president
    7. Articles of impeachment
    8. The resignation
  C. The aftermath of Watergate
    1. Ford's selection
    2. The Nixon pardon
    3. Distrust of leaders and institutions
    4. Shock at the crudity of leaders
    5. Resiliency of American institutions
    6. War Powers Act
    7. Campaign financing legislation
    8. Freedom of Information Act

VII. Reforms of the seventies
  A. The women's movement
    1. Roots of the movement
    2. Role of Betty Friedan
    3. Civil Rights Act
    4. Affirmative Action
    5. Abortions and coeducation
    6. The Equal Rights Amendment
    7. Future prospects for the women's movement
  B. Hispanics

1. Role of Cesar Chavez and the UFW
2. The Hispanic population
3. Important issues
C. Native Americans
   1. Reasons for emergence of Indian rights
   2. Militant tactics
   3. Court actions against treaty violations
D. The environmental movement
   1. Recognition of the limits of growth
   2. Impact of the energy crisis
   3. Competition with vested interests
   4. Reasons for opposition to environmental reform
      a. Cost
      b. Loss of faith in governmental efforts
      c. Refusal to accept lesser standard of living

VIII. The Ford presidency
  A. Drift at the end of the Nixon administration
  B. Ford's battle with the economy
  C. Foreign policy accomplishments
  D. The election of 1976
    1. Ford's nomination
    2. Reasons for the Carter rise
    3. Carter's victory

IX. The Carter presidency
  A. The Carter style and his challenges
  B. Early domestic moves
    1. Appointments
    2. Amnesty for draft dodgers
    3. Administrative reorganization
    4. Environmental legislation
    5. Deregulation of the oil industry

6. The crisis of confidence
C. Foreign policy initiatives
   1. Human rights focus
   2. Panama Canal Treaties
   3. Diplomatic relations with China
   4. The Camp David Accords
D. Failure to manage the economy
   1. Emphasis on reducing unemployment
   2. A reversal: the reduction of government deficits
E. The SALT II negotiations
F. Reactions to the invasion of Afghanistan
G. The Iranian Crisis
   1. Background to the seizure
   2. Carter's efforts to help the hostages
   3. The crisis ended
H. The election of 1980
   1. Reagan's background
   2. Aids to Reagan's election
      a. An older population
      b. Shift to the Sunbelt
      c. Revival of evangelical religion
      d. Disenchantment with Carter
   3. The election results

X. The Reagan presidency
  A. The Reagan stance and style
  B. Reaganomics
  C. The growth of budget deficits
  D. A stronger stance in foreign affairs
  E. The Polish revolts
  F. Actions in Central America
  G. Rekindling the mood of the 1950s

KEY ITEMS OF CHRONOLOGY

Betty Friedan's *The Feminine Mystique* published	1963
My Lai massacre	1968
Cambodian "incursion"	April 1970
Swann v. Charlotte-Mecklenburg Board of Education	1971
Pentagon Papers published	June 1971
Nixon's visit to China	February 1972
SALT agreement signed	May 1972
Watergate break-in occurred	June 1972
Last American troops left Vietnam	March 1973

Nixon's resignation	Aug. 9, 1974
South Vietnam fell to the North	April 1975
Bakke v. Board of Regents of California	1978
Camp David Agreement	September 1978
Iranian Hostages held	November 1979–January 1981

TERMS TO MASTER

Listed below are some important terms or people with which you should be familiar after you complete the study of this chapter. Explain the significance of each name or term.

1. fragging
2. My Lai massacre
3. *Pentagon Papers*
4. "Middle America"
5. *Swann v. Charlotte-Mecklenburg Board of Education*
6. *Bakke v. Board of Regents of California*
7. Revenue Sharing
8. Spiro Agnew
9. OPEC
10. SALT
11. George McGovern
12. Watergate
13. Saturday Night Massacre
14. ERA
15. Stagflation
16. Henry Kissinger
17. War Powers Act
18. Camp David Agreements
19. Iranian hostages
20. Reaganomics

VOCABULARY BUILDING

Listed below are some words or phrases used in this chapter. Look up each word in your dictionary unless the meaning is given here.

1. tocsin
2. vacillation
3. capricious
4. duplicity
5. lamentation
6. détente

EXERCISES FOR UNDERSTANDING

When you have completed the reading of the chapter, answer each of the following questions. If you have difficulty, go back and reread the section of the chapter related to the question.

Multiple-Choice Questions

Select the letter of the response which best completes the statement.

1. Nixon sought to lessen criticism of the Vietnam War by
   A. slowly reducing the number of American troops there
   B. creating a lottery to determine who would be drafted
   C. using more air strikes rather than ground warfare
   D. all of the above

2. According to the text, Nixon's delay of the peace settlement from October 1972 to January 1973 resulted in
   A. an agreement that North Vietnam would remove its troops from South Vietnam
   B. a cooling-off period for the people of North Vietnam
   C. a willingness for South Vietnam finally to accept the same terms offered in October
   D. an agreement by North Vietnam finally to surrender

3. Nixon's chief link to Middle America was
   A. Daniel Moynihan
   B. Robert Finch
   C. Spiro Agnew
   D. the ambassador to Mexico

4. On civil rights, the Burger Court
   A. gave decisions of which Nixon approved

B. continued to press for school integration and even approved busing
C. refused to permit busing within a unified school district
D. ordered a return to the concept of neighborhood schools

5. McGovern won his nomination
A. because he seemed to be the most conservative national Democrat to oppose Nixon
B. primarily with the help of party regulars
C. because he was an outsider who had no connections with Washington
D. because of Democratic party reforms which increased the number of minority delegates

6. Nixon was accused in Watergate of *all but which one* of the following?
A. obstructing justice through paying witnesses to remain silent
B. defying Congress by withholding the tapes
C. using federal agencies to deprive citizens of their rights
D. stealing funds from the reelection campaign

7. Betty Friedan launched the women's movement with claims that women
A. were too educated to dabble in politics
B. deserved equality with men in all areas
C. should be permitted to serve in the armed forces
D. were bored with housework and childcare

8. To deal with the economy, Carter first sought to
A. deregulate the airlines and trucking industries
B. balance the federal budget
C. reduce taxes
D. reduce unemployment

True-False Questions

Indicate whether each statement is true or false.

1. The Cambodian "incursion" led to widespread rioting on American college campuses.
2. Two years after the Vietnam War ended, North Vietnam took control of the South.
3. Nixon's welfare reform involved direct payments of a guaranteed annual income of $1,600 to poor families.
4. Nixon used wage and price controls to stem inflation.
5. The War Powers Act requires a president to withdraw troops sent abroad after sixty days unless specifically authorized by Congress for a longer stay.
6. By the 1970s support for environmental causes was growing.
7. Carter stressed a foreign policy of pragmatism rather than supporting a fixed policy based on principle.
8. Reaganomics includes tax reductions and elimination of federal deficits.

Essay Questions

1. How did Nixon's Vietnam War policies compare with Johnson's?
2. Discuss the impact of the Vietnam War on American society.
3. What were the aims and accomplishments of Nixon's domestic policy?
4. Trace the course of America's economic problems from 1970 to 1983.
5. How important were Nixon's diplomatic achievements with China and Russia? Could a Democrat have achieved the same gains? Explain.
6. Explain Nixon's wrongdoing in the Watergate episode. How do you assess the charges leveled against him by the House Judiciary Committee? How did Watergate compare with the scandals of the Harding and Grant administrations?
7. Discuss the reaction to President Ford's pardon of Nixon.
8. How would you compare Jimmy Carter's foreign and domestic policies to those of Woodrow Wilson.
9. Account for the election of Ronald Reagan. How did his policies differ from those of his recent predecessors?

DOCUMENTS

Document 1. The Charges against Nixon

When the House Judiciary Committee completed its investigation and voted the impeachment of Nixon in July 1974, there were three articles which obtained a majority vote of the committee. The heart of the three articles is excerpted here.

Article I. In his conduct of the office of President of the United States, Richard M. Nixon, in violation of his constitutional oath faithfully to execute the office of President of the United States and, to the best of his ability, preserve, protect, and defend the Constitution of the United States, and in violation of his constitutional duty to take care that the laws be faithfully executed, has prevented, obstructed, and impeded the administration of justice, . . . Richard M. Nixon, using the powers of his high office, engaged personally and through his subordinates and agents, in a course of conduct or plan designed to delay, impede, and obstruct the investigation of such unlawful entry; to cover up, conceal and protect those responsible; and to conceal the existence and scope of other unlawful covert activities. . . .

Article II.   . . . Richard M. Nixon . . . has repeatedly engaged in conduct violating the constitutional rights of citizens, impairing the due and proper administration of justice and the conduct of lawful inquiries, or contravening the laws governing agencies of the executive branch and the purpose of these agencies. . . .

Article III. Richard M. Nixon, contrary to his oath faithfully to execute the office of President of the United States . . . has failed without lawful cause or excuse to produce papers and things as directed by duly authorized subpoenas issued by the Committee on the Judiciary of the House of Representatives on April 11, 1974, May 15, 1974, May 30, 1974, and June 24, 1974, and willfully disobeying such subpoenas. . . . In refusing to produce these papers and things, Richard M. Nixon, substituting his judgment as to what materials were necessary for the inquiry, interposed the powers of the Presidency against the lawful subpoenas of the House of Representatives, thereby assuming to himself functions and judgments necessary to the exercise of the sole power of impeachment vested by the Constitution in the House of Representatives.

[U.S. Congress, House of Representatives, *Report of the Committee on the Judiciary*, 93rd Cong., 2d sess., 1974, pp.]

Document 2. Sen. Sam Ervin Explains the Meaning and Consequences of Watergate

Prior to the report quoted above, the Ervin Committee of the Senate had throughout the summer of 1973 treated the American public to weeks of televised hearings at which various Watergate conspirators had testified about the labyrinthine developments of the Watergate affair. In June 1974, shortly before the House Judiciary Committee moved to impeach Nixon, the Ervin Committee made its report. Accompanying the report was a statement from Senator Ervin in which he tried to summarize the Watergate episode in a few paragraphs. Because the report was made prior to the House committee's decision to move toward impeachment of the president,

Ervin began his report with a disclaimer to indicate that he was not trying to pass judgment on the president's guilt in the matter. His report is a succinct statement of the Watergate affair and a comment on its implications for the future.

I am not undertaking to usurp and exercise the power of impeachment, which the Constitution confers upon the House of Representatives alone. As a consequence, nothing I say should be construed as an expression of an opinion in respect to the question of whether or not President Nixon is impeachable in connection with the Watergate or any other matter. . . .

I shall also refrain from making any comment on the question of whether or not the President has performed in an acceptable manner his paramount constitutional obligation "to take care that the laws be faithfully executed."

Watergate was not invented by enemies of the Nixon administration or even by the news media. On the contrary, Watergate was perpetrated upon America by White House and political aides, whom President Nixon himself had entrusted with the management of his campaign for reelection to the Presidency, a campaign which was divorced to a marked degree from the campaigns of other Republicans who sought election to public office in 1972. I note at this point without elaboration that these White House and political aides were virtually without experience in either Government or politics apart from their association with President Nixon.

5. Watergate was without precedent in the political annals of America in respect to the scope and intensity of its unethical and illegal actions. To be sure, there had been previous milder political scandals in American history. That fact does not excuse Watergate. Murder and stealing have occurred in every generation since Earth began, but that fact has not made murder meritorious or larceny legal.

What Was Watergate?

Watergate was a conglomerate of various illegal and unethical activities in which various officers and employees of the Nixon reelection committee and various White House aides of President Nixon participated in varying ways and degrees to accomplish these successive objectives:

1. To destroy, insofar as the Presidential election of 1972 was concerned, the integrity of the process by which the President of the United States is nominated and elected.

2. To hide from law enforcement officers, prosecutors, grand jurors, courts, the news media, and the American people the identities and wrongdoing of those officers and employees of the Nixon reelection committees, and those White House aides who had undertaken to destroy the integrity of the process by which the President of the United States is nominated and elected.

To accomplish the first of these objectives. . . .

1. They exacted enormous contributions—usually in cash—from corporate executives by impliedly implanting in their minds the impressions that the making of the contributions was necessary to

insure that the corporations would receive governmental favors, or avoid governmental disfavors, while President Nixon remained in the White House. A substantial portion of the contributions were made out of corporate funds in violation of a law enacted by Congress a generation ago.

2. They hid substantial parts of these contributions in cash in safes and safe deposits to conceal their sources and the identities of those who had made them.

3. They disbursed substantial portions of these hidden contributions in a surreptitious manner to finance the bugging and the burglary of the offices of the Democratic National Committee in the Watergate complex in Washington. . . .

4. They deemed the departments and agencies of the Federal Government to be the political playthings of the Nixon administration rather than impartial instruments for serving the people, and undertook to induce them to channel Federal contracts, grants, and loans to areas, groups, or individuals so as to promote the reelection of the President rather than to further the welfare of the people.

5. They branded as enemies of the President individuals and members of the news media who dissented from the President's policies and opposed his reelection, and conspired to urge the Department of Justice, the Federal Bureau of Investigation, the Internal Revenue Service, and the Federal Communications Commission to pervert the use of their legal powers to harass them for so doing.

6. They borrowed from the Central Intelligence Agency disguises which E. Howard Hunt used in political espionage operations, and photographic equipment which White House employees known as the "Plumbers" and their hired confederates used in connection with burglarizing the office of a psychiatrist which they believed contained information concerning Daniel Ellsberg which the White House was anxious to secure.

7. They assigned to E. Howard Hunt, who was at the time a White House consultant occupying an office in the Executive Office Building, the gruesome task of falsifying State Department documents which they contemplated using in their altered state to discredit the Democratic Party by defaming the memory of former President John Fitzgerald Kennedy, who as the hapless victim of an assassin's bullet had been sleeping in the tongueless silence of the dreamless dust for 9 years.

8. They used campaign funds to hire saboteurs to forge and disseminate false and scurrilous libels of honorable men running for the Democratic Presidential nomination in Democratic Party primaries.

During the darkness of the early morning of June 17, 1972, James W. McCord, the security chief of the John Mitchell committee, and four residents of Miami, Fla., were arrested by Washington police while they were burglarizing the offices of the Democratic National Committee in the Watergate complex to obtain political intelligence. . . .

The arrest of McCord and the four residents of Miami created consternation in the Nixon reelection committees and the White

House. . . . various White House aides undertook to conceal from law enforcement officers, prosecutors, grand jurors, courts, the news media, and the American people the identities and activities of those officers and employees of the Nixon reelection committee and those White House aides who had participated in any way in the Watergate affair . . .

1. They destroyed the records of the Nixon reelection committee antedating the bugging and the burglary.

2. They induced the Acting Director of the FBI, who was a Nixon appointee, to destroy the State Department documents which E. Howard Hunt had been falsifying.

3. They obtained from the Acting Director of the FBI copies of the scores of interviews conducted by the FBI agents in connection with their investigation of the bugging and the burglary, and were enabled thereby to coach their confederates to give false and misleading statements to the FBI.

4. They sought to persuade the FBI to refrain from investigating the sources of the campaign funds which were used to finance the bugging and the burglary.

5. They intimidated employees of the Nixon reelection committees and employees of the White House by having their lawyers present when these employees were being questioned by agents of the FBI, and thus deterred these employees from making full disclosures to the FBI.

6. They lied to agents of the FBI, prosecutors, and grand jurors who undertook to investigate the bugging and the burglary, and to Judge Sirica and the petit jurors who tried the seven original Watergate defendants in January, 1973.

7. They persuaded the Department of Justice and the prosecutors to take out-of-court statements from Maurice Stans, President Nixon's chief campaign fundraiser, and Charles Colson, Egil Krogh, and David Young, White House aides, and Charles Colson's secretary, instead of requiring them to testify before the grand jury investigating the bugging and the burglary in conformity with established procedures governing such matters, and thus denied the grand jurors the opportunity to question them.

8. They persuaded the Department of Justice and the prosecutors to refrain from asking Donald Segretti, their chief hired saboteur, any questions involving Herbert W. Kalmbach, the President's personal attorney, who was known by them to have paid Segretti for dirty tricks he perpetrated upon honorable men seeking the Democratic Presidential nomination. . . .

9. They made cash payments totaling hundreds of thousands of dollars out of campaign funds in surreptitious ways to the seven original Watergate defendants as hush money to buy their silence. . . .

10. They gave assurances to some of the original seven defendants that they would receive Presidential clemency after serving short portions of their sentences if they refrained from divulging the identities and activities of the officers and employees of the Nixon reelection committees and the White House aides who had participated in the Watergate affair.

11. They made arrangements by which the attorneys who represented the seven original Watergate defendants received their fees in cash from moneys which had been collected to finance President Nixon's reelection campaign.

12. They induced the Department of Justice and the prosecutors of the seven original Watergate defendants to assure the news media and the general public that there was no evidence that any persons other than the seven original Watergate defendants were implicated in any way in the Watergate-related crimes.

13. They inspired massive efforts on the part of segments of the news media friendly to the administration to persuade the American people that most of the members of the Select Committee named by the Senate to investigate the Watergate were biased and irresponsible men motivated solely by desires to exploit the matters they investigated for personal or partisan advantage. . . .

One shudders to think that the Watergate conspiracies might have been effectively concealed and their most dramatic episode might have been dismissed as a "third-rate" burglary conceived and committed solely by the seven original Watergate defendants had it not been for the courage and penetrating understanding of Judge Sirica, the thoroughness of the investigative reporting of Carl Bernstein, Bob Woodward, and the other representatives of the free press, the labors of the Senate Select Committee and its excellent staff, and the dedication and diligence of Special Prosecutors Archibald Cox and Leon Jarworski and their associates.

Why Was Watergate?

Unlike the men who were responsible for Teapot Dome, the Presidential aides who perpetrated Watergate were not seduced by the love of money, which is sometimes thought to be the root of all evil. On the contrary, they were instigated by a lust for political power, which is at least as corrupting as political power itself. . . .

They knew that the power they enjoyed would be lost and the policies to which they adhered would be frustrated if the President should be defeated.

As a consequence of these things, they believed the President's reelection to be a most worthy objective, and succombed to an age-old temptation. They resorted to evil means to promote what they conceived to be a good end.

Their lust for political power blinded them to ethical considerations and legal requirements; to Aristotle's aphorism that the good of man must be the end of politics; and to Grover Cleveland's conviction that a public office is a public trust.

They had forgotten, if they ever knew, that the Constitution is designed to be a law for rulers and people alike at all times and under all circumstances; and that no doctrine involving more pernicious consequences to the commonweal has ever been invented by the wit of man than the notion that any of its provisions can be suspended by the President for any reason whatsoever.

On the contrary, they apparently believed that the President is above the Constitution, and has the autocratic power to suspend its provisions if he decides in his own unreviewable judgment that his action in so doing promotes his own political interests or the welfare of the Nation. . . .

The Antidote for Future Watergates

Is there an antidote which will prevent future Watergates? If so, what is it? . . .

Candor compels the confession . . . that law alone will not suffice to prevent future Watergates. . . .

Law is not self-executing. Unfortunately, at times its execution rests in the hands of those who are faithless to it. And even when its enforcement is committed to those who revere it, law merely deters some human beings from offending, and punishes other human beings for offending. It does not make men good. This task can be performed only by ethics or religion or morality. . . .

When all is said, the only sure antidote for future Watergates is understanding of fundamental principles and intellectual and moral integrity in the men and women who achieve or are entrusted with governmental political power.

[U.S. Congress, Senate, Select Committee on Presidential Campaign Activities, *Final Report*, 93rd Cong., 2d sess., 1974, pp. 1097–1103]

Questions for Reflection

The United States Constitution in Article II, Section 4, states that the President "shall be removed from office on impeachment for, and on conviction of, treason, bribery, or other high crimes and misdemeanors." Do you consider the crimes of which Nixon was accused impeachable offenses? Why or why not?

Why was Ervin so careful to disavow any indictment of the president in his report? Based on the charges of the House Rules Committee in Document 1, which of the actions attributed to others by Ervin might have been charged to the president also?

Who benefited from the Watergate crimes? Were monetary considerations at the heart of the Watergate crimes? Is a president who is dutifully exercising his responsibilities "above the Constitution" with the power to suspend its provisions when he needs to do so? Explain.

What and/or who does Ervin credit with bringing the Watergate conspirators to justice? What does the case suggest about the need for an independent judiciary and a free press? How do you react to Ervin's prescription for preventing future Watergates?

ANSWERS TO MULTIPLE-CHOICE AND TRUE-FALSE QUESTIONS

Multiple-Choice Questions

1-D, 2-C, 3-C, 4-B, 5-D, 6-D, 7-D, 8-D

True-False Questions

1-T, 2-T, 3-T, 4-T, 5-T, 6-T, 7-F, 8-F